Managing Democracy in Central America

A Case Study:
United States Election Supervision in Nicaragua, 1927-1933

North·South Center
U N I V E R S I T Y   O F   M I A M I

Managing Democracy in Central America

A Case Study:
United States Election Supervision in Nicaragua, 1927-1933

Thomas J. Dodd

JL
1618
.D63
1992

DISTRIBUTED BY

LYNNE RIENNER PUBLISHERS

1800 30TH ST., SUITE 314, BOULDER, CO 80301
TEL: 303-444-6684 · FAX: 303-444-0824

THE NORTH-SOUTH CENTER promotes, through cultural and technical exchange, better relations among the United States, Canada, and the nations of Latin America and the Caribbean. The Center provides a disciplined, intellectual focus for improved relations, commerce, and understanding between North America and Latin America. The Center conducts programs of education, training, cooperative study, public outreach, and research and engages in an active program of publication and dissemination of information on the Americas. The North-South Center fosters linkages among academic and research institutions throughout the Americas and acts as an agent of change in the region.

North-South Center, University of Miami

Ambler H. Moss, Jr.	Kathleen A. Hamman	Mary M. Mapes
Director	Editorial Director	Publications Director
Jaime Suchlicki	Ivy Fleischer Kupec	Stephanie True Moss
Executive Director	Editor	Assoc. Publications Dir.

ISBN-1-56000-631-5
Printed in the United States of America

Photos courtesy of the Still Pictures Branch, United States National Archives.

Library of Congress **Cataloging-in-Publication-Data**

Dodd, Thomas J.
    Managing Democracy in Central America: A Case Study. United States election supervision in Nicaragua. 1927-1933/ Thomas J. Dodd.
        p.   cm.
    ISBN 1-56000-631-5 (pbk.) : $18.95
        1. Elections—Nicaragua—History—20th century. 2. Election monitoring—Nicaragua—History—20th century. 3. Nicaragua—Foreign relations—United States—History—20th century. 4. United States—Foreign Relations—Nicaragua—History—20th century. 5. Nicaragua—Politics and government—1909-1937. I. Title.
JL1618.D63 1992
324.97285' 051 — dc20   92-26327
                                                                    CIP

FTW
AHH6676

Today this is a struggle of the Nicaraguan people, in general, to expel the foreign invasion of my country....The only way to put an end to this struggle is the immediate withdrawal of the invading forces from our territory...and supervising the coming elections by representatives of Latin America instead of by [North] American marines.

> Country and Liberty,
> Augusto César (A.C.) Sandino
> San Rafael, (Nicaragua) February 3, 1928

...the purpose of our action, far from being in derogation of the rights and interests of Nicaragua as a sovereign and independent state, is to promote [that] independence and sovereignty in the most effective way. We are to assist her to hold for the first time in her history as a republic a free and fair election of her president. She has asked us to do this; ...can anyone say that this great constructive step is an impairment of her sovereignty?

> Henry L. Stimson,
> *American Policy in Nicaragua* (1927)

Contents

Acknowledgments

The author is grateful to a number of people who helped me gain access to important documents in both the United States and Nicaraguan archives. The patience of Julia Carroll, former reference consultant in the State Department Records Division, and Ronald Hise and Patricia Dowling, archivists, was invaluable. Dr. Vincente Navas, former chairman of the Nicaraguan National Election Board, provided me with Supreme Electoral Tribunal records in Managua. He also offered his own considerable information and insight concerning Nicaraguan political figures who worked on election boards and participated in Liberal and Conservative party meetings from 1928 to 1932.

Moreover, the late Emiliano Chamorro granted this writer interviews in 1965, offering personal recollections regarding his activities in this era of election supervision. Through several discussions, many Sandino followers in Northern Nicaragua recalled their guerrilla campaigns in several discussions, which helped to reconstruct the election supervision story.

The author conducted a considerable portion of this book's research in Nicaragua. The United States ambassador to the republic, Aaron S. Brown, arranged interviews with many people who were active participants in the country's politics from 1927 to 1932. This writer is indebted to him for his many helpful suggestions and good counsel. Special thanks are also due to the staff of the Ministry of Gobernación, which contained material on election board deliberations. Countless veterans of the Sandino movement, especially those who operated near local election supervision operations, helped me assess the effectiveness of the election boards' procedures.

A number of Nicaraguan journalists provided materials covering major political events during the election. Most helpful were Joaquín Zavala Urtecho, editor of *La Revista del Pensamiento Centroamericano*, grandson of President Joaquín

i

Zavala (1879-1883), and Orlando Cuadra Downing, a member of the editorial staff of the same periodical and a grandson of President Vicente Cuadra (1871-1875). Both helped me work on various materials concerning the history of the Conservative and Liberal parties. Portions of this work later appeared in *La Revista del Pensamiento Centroamericano.*

Finally, the author wishes to pay a special note of appreciation to Dr. Peter Krogh, dean of the School of Foreign Service of Georgetown University, for his constant encouragement and help on this project.

Preface

Civil war rages in Nicaragua. Armed rebels resist the authority of a central government, and political rivals vie for power in Managua. A peace plan proposes democratization through amnesty, free elections, and the creation of a non-partisan military. The United States has intervened to end the expansion of radical policies from Nicaragua to the rest of Central America. The chief executive in this Nicaraguan embroilment, Violeta Barrios de Chamorro, is a member of a prominent family, a major force in the country's political history. While these conditions reflect a contemporary crisis in 1990, they also resemble an earlier time, 1927-1933, when the United States tried to end Nicaragua's continuous civil wars and political partisanship through supervised elections.[1]

The resignation in 1926 of President Emiliano Chamorro, a distant relative of Violeta Barrios de Chamorro, was largely precipitated by the United States' intervention. The strategy in 1927 to bring an end to internal strife and legitimacy in elections accelerated the United States' intervention militarily. It also precipitated congressional opposition to the project by cutting off financial assistance as it did during the 1980s. Rebels under the leadership of a liberal party dissident, Augusto César Sandino, opposed the United States' actions from 1927 to 1933. Sandino, a sympathizer of revolutionary Mexico was perceived as a Marxist. After a bitter military conflict with the United States, they were finally persuaded in 1933 to settle in designated rural areas where they could live, police themselves, and participate in municipal government. Today's Contras have posed an equally contentious challenge to President Violeta Chamorro. Yet they too have finally agreed to settle in specific sections of the country with their own rural

---

[1] The New York Times, 9 April 1990, p.18

police force, making political decisions for themselves.

Continuous civil wars and political division as well as a prominent United States presence still characterizes Nicaraguan contemporary history. The country has made a full circle from 1927-1933 to the present. The years 1927 and 1990 are connected. They are pivotal years that mark efforts to end unbroken cycles of military and political conflict in this Central American nation. The political heirs of Sandino today, the Sandinista National Liberation Front, came to power in a 1979 revolution, ending the Somoza family's 40-year dictatorial rule. The rise of Anastasio Somoza Garcia began during the United States' 1927-1933 intervention. And in 1990, the Sandinistas turned power over to a Chamorro in an internationally monitored election.

A civil war began in the early 1980s as an outgrowth of the 1979 revolution led by the Contras, a counterrevolutionary, anti-Sandinista force whose leaders were Somoza loyalists. The conflict contributed to an outbreak again of Nicaragua's pattern of political conflict. This time a general peace for Central America, by which internal reconciliation was necessary in Nicaragua, was drawn up by Costa Rican President Oscar Arias. The plan called for amnesty of all political prisoners, disarmament, and democratization in the electoral process. The United States promoted these same goals in its 1927 military intervention.

This work examines a United States' effort to bring an end to violent civil strife in Nicaragua during the late 1920s and early 1930s. It was a diplomatic experiment that included direct military action and election supervision, a dual strategy to create a government which a majority of Nicaraguans could accept. Unfortunately, its legacy was the Somoza dictatorship, 1936 to 1979. In February 1990, the electoral defeat of the Sandinistas to Violeta Chamorro de Barrios marked the first time since 1932 that power had been transferred peacefully to an opposition. As in the 1927-1933 era, the United States was still concerned with Nicaragua's ability to end a civil war, create a nonpartisan military, and find a place for rebel forces in the political process.

These strictly internal Nicaraguan problems have generally dominated the nature of United States relations with all of Central America. Always a potential site for a transisthmian canal before and after the completed construction of a waterway across Panama in 1914, Managua suffered domestic political feuding that raised the constant specter of its impact on regional stability. The United States' attention was frequently riveted toward Nicaragua from the advent of the Monroe Doctrine in 1823 and especially after the Mexican War in 1845. Its strategic interests in the Atlantic Caribbean and later in the Asian Pacific were secured by politically stable and friendly governments in Central America, particularly Nicaragua, as an Isthmian passageway. As a consequence, nationalism and popular resistance interventions have been expressed frequently by Nicaraguan leaders from mid-nineteenth century through the Sandinista Revolution of 1979. These movements have been consistently perceived as a threat to United States regional and global security interests. Managua has often been the catalyst for people supporting regional stability and promoting friendly ties to the United States as well as eras which have challenged the Monroe Doctrine, promoting nationalism and rejecting Washington's intervention.

Nicaragua's pantheon of heroes all reflect efforts to curb foreign intervention from the Indian hero Diriangén in the sixteenth century to Augusto César Sandino in the late 1920s and 1930s. His political heirs, the Sandinistas, have been the most recent example of strident nationalism and anti-Yankee feeling in the revolution of 1979.

Paradoxically, some Nicaraguan leaders since its independence have built their power base on the military and political presence of the United States in the country's internal affairs. The 40-year Somoza family rule (1936-1979) attests to this phenomena. Consequently, Nicaragua's political process has often been polarized, extending to civil wars. Frequently, the United States has chosen its allies among these warring factions, thereby deepening and worsening political antagonisms.

The year 1927 marked a brief episode, an effort to end a civil war, depoliticize an army, and establish mechanisms for holding free elections and hopefully creating stability through democracy. Political peace was needed in a nation which might in the future provide another transit site for the United States. From 1927 until 1933, Washington's role in Nicaragua's domestic affairs remained unresolved, as it does today in a new era of tested democracy both in Nicaragua and Central America.

I

A Background for Conflict:
President Calvin Coolidge
Looks South

THE REPUBLIC OF NICARAGUA has had a long and difficult experience in political development partly because of deep partisan conflicts within its borders and partly because of outside interference by states which have had a special interest in a transisthmian route through Central America.

Soon after its independence in the nineteenth century, this largest of Central American states was plagued by serious domestic problems, many of which had begun in the colonial period. Quarrels between factions and family clans supporting separation from Spain and others advocating the maintenance of Castile's colonial empire eventually became Conservative and Liberal parties contending for power. Their feuds were not based on ideological or class differences. Yet, as a country of city dwellers, Nicaragua's concentration of people in two or three western, urban areas heightened differences between the commercial interests of León's Liberals and the Conservative agricultural elite in Granada. Consequently, political alignments in the nation centered almost exclusively around the economic goals of two municipalities. The selection of Managua as the republic's capital was sanctioned largely because Liberals and Conservatives refused to accept the seat of government in the other's region.[1]

After the breakup of the Central American Federation (1823-1838), Nicaragua faced serious military and economic intrusions from outside forces which in turn did little to mollify the bitter conflicts in its domestic affairs. The Liberal and

---

[1] José Coronel Urtecho, *Reflexiones sobre la Historia de Nicaragua* 1 (Managua: Imprenta Nacional, 1963), 10.

Conservative parties had more in common with their counterparts in the rest of Central America than with one another in their own country, thereby inviting interference in the country's internal affairs. Great Britain had taken an interest in this strip of land between the Atlantic and Pacific Oceans and sanctioned numerous forays by its naval officers in this outpost of Spain's colonial empire early in the sixteenth century. While British economic activities grew along the republic's east (Mosquito) coast, Liberal and Conservative party leaders oftentimes sought help from the "mistress of the seas" as they contended for power.

The United States began to play a significant role in Nicaragua's political embroilments in the aftermath of the Mexican War in 1848. In the early 1850s, the Liberals became involved in a struggle to oust the entrenched Conservatives from power and looked with special favor upon the exploits of William Walker, the United States soldier of fortune and filibusterer, as a force who might assist them. Before long, the Liberals realized they had committed a tactical error by asking the Yankee adventurer for help as he eventually became president of the republic in 1856.

Fortunately for Nicaraguans, the "Yankee president" feuded with Cornelius Vanderbilt, the New York financier and owner of the Accessory Transit Company that operated steamship transportation between the country's Atlantic and Pacific coasts. Vanderbilt was able to bring about Walker's downfall in 1857 by supplying arms to his opponents. Nicaragua then began a long period under successive Conservative regimes lasting until 1893.

When José Santos Zelaya became president in 1893, beginning a 16-year rule, a new constitution was promulgated, and his followers looked forward to the implementation of many reforms. The Zelaya era began Nicaragua's modernization (1893-1909) and provided significant improvement in both the nation's domestic problems and its influence in Central American politics. For example, he was able to obtain Great Britain's recognition of the nation's sovereignty in the east coast Mosquito region. He encouraged foreign investment from both the United States and Western Europe.

After the Spanish-American War (1898) and Panama's independence (1903), United States strategic interests increased considerably in Central America. When Zelaya rejected outright the United State's bid for sole management over a future canal through Nicaragua, the president faced U.S.

opposition. His relations with the United States worsened when he readily offered Japan exclusive rights to build an interoceanic canal and meddled in Central American states' internal affairs.

Conservatives and disenchanted Liberals revolted against the Nicaraguan chief executive in 1909, and the United States government looked favorably on efforts to oust him. When Zelaya tried to retain control, the United States rejected his hand-picked successor and refused to recognize him. The failure of the Liberal party to win North American approval was to have far-reaching effects on Nicaragua's politics. Soon Juan Estrada, a Conservative rebel leader and governor of the eastern department of Bluefields, secured complete control over the republic and won U.S. recognition. Washington intervened diplomatically to settle the country's political disputes and establish financial control. The U.S. government was convinced that if Nicaragua's fiscal policies were managed properly, political stability would emerge. In any case, the Conservative regime led by Juan Estrada (1910-1911) agreed to U.S. financial supervision by accepting a loan from a consortium of North American bankers in June 1911, ultimately giving them a 51 percent stake in the Banco Nacional de Nicaragua. As security for this arrangement, a customs collectorship was established and operated by an American Collector General. By 1912, the United States and the Conservatives had developed such a convenient and accommodating relationship that Brown Brothers and Company and J. and W. Seligman and Company of New York granted the Conservatives a $1.5 million loan to assume the debt Nicaragua owed to Europeans, now payable to the United States. This payment was guaranteed by turning over the country's customs receipts to the United States. As a result, the incumbent Conservative party, which accepted the financial agreement, was recognized and supported politically as the country's best prospect for maintaining internal peace. This was to be a principal axiom in United States Nicaraguan policy for some time.

Simply because the Conservative party had been installed as the official caretaker of Nicaraguan stability, peace was not forthcoming. For example, personal rivalries among Conservatives plagued the country. So in September 1912, the United States placed a marine detachment in Nicaragua for the express purpose of insuring the continued leadership of President Adolfo Díaz, who was subsequently reelected in November of the same year. Prospects for the construction of a second interoceanic canal across Nicaragua increased when the Panama project was completed in 1914. As a result, the U.S. government watched the course of the country's domestic politics closely.

While the financial problems of Nicaragua were being settled under the Conservative regimes of Díaz and his successor, the colorful and intrepid Emiliano Chamorro (President, 1917-1921, 1926), no progress had been made in reducing the powerful position of the chief executive in the nation's electoral process. Almost by tradition, Nicaraguan presidents were able to control the election of their successors primarily through fraud and intimidation. While it provided for a relatively smooth continuation of Conservative rule from 1911 on, it enhanced the vast powers of the country's chief magistrates and reduced chances for the "out party" to defeat the incumbent government through the electoral process.

Even though Emiliano Chamorro, who had emerged as a major political figure after Zelaya's fall in 1909, had effectively demonstrated his ability as president to maintain order in the republic from 1917 on, plans for retaining control through his uncle and chosen successor Diego Chamorro in 1920 prompted the United States to pay closer attention to the problem of "*continuismo*" or perpetuation of political power. Therefore, the U.S. government dispatched a U.S. Army major to act as an observer in the 1920 presidential contest. Chamorro saw this special mission as a veiled threat to his plans for keeping his party in control.[2] As a result, he instituted some minor electoral reforms. As usual, the Liberals charged that the election was replete with fraudulent practices and failed to obtain any assistance from the United States in altering their political prospects. Diego Chamorro took office in 1921 and the United States election observer reported that a most ingenious and effective president had managed to place his own choice in office while simultaneously continuing to wield great power in the republic.

Not long after the 1920 election, the United States informed Nicaragua that its electoral process needed reform. Among the system's most glaring weaknesses — the governing party unfairly supervised voter registration and election-day balloting.

Harold Dodds, a United States citizen, a political science professor, and the secretary of the National Municipal League,

_____

[2] Emiliano Chamorro, interview, Managua, March 25, 1965.

drew up an electoral law that the Nicaraguan Congress approved in 1923. It required all election boards to have Liberal as well as Conservative representatives. While the new measure made some inroads in the republic's electoral process, it did not remove the entrenched Conservatives from office. When President Chamorro died in late 1923, the Conservative party was still able to regain full control of the nation. In fact, the deceased president's nephew, Emiliano, later was able to maneuver Conservative President Carlos Solórzano and Liberal Vice-President Juan Bautista Sacasa out of office in January 1926 and to reclaim the presidency.

This was a fateful step for Chamorro. The action began a process which was ultimately to dislodge the Conservative party in 1928. The former president and maker of Nicaraguan chief executives not only incurred U.S. disfavor but precipitated a Liberal revolt which was to bring all the republic's political ills to the world's attention again. When Emiliano Chamorro staged a coup, ousting President Solórzano in 1926, he also denied Juan Bautista Sacasa, the Liberal vice-president who had joined the coalition government, his right to the presidency.

This was the closest a Liberal had come to the chief magistrate's office in a long time. The able, proud Sacasa was not about to watch this opportunity pass. He began a military campaign with a proclamation of a constitutional government on December 2, 1926, to obtain the Nicaraguan presidency. According to Chamorro, the United States promised to back him for president in 1928.[3,4] Even though Washington saw the need to preserve legitimacy by ousting Chamorro, it was not prepared to allow the Liberals to take office through an armed

---

[3] Ibid.

[4] The Coolidge Administration later gathered evidence from a wide range of sources which together convinced government officials that Mexico was assisting Juan Bautista Sacasa and Augusto César Sandino. United States Consuls in Veracruz, Mexico; Puerto Castilla, Honduras; and Military Intelligence Branch G-2, Fort Sam Houston, Texas, to the State Department, June 1928, 817.00/5544, 817/5549, 871.00/5616, Records of the Department of the Army, Military Intelligence G-2, National Archives. Pro-Sandino groups were also identified in Mexico as suppliers of arms to the Nicaraguan rebels, among them, "Manos Fuera de Nicaragua": Secretary of the Navy to Secretary of State, April 13, 1928, 817.00/5564, Records of the State Department, National Archives.

rebellion. Consequently, the United States withheld recognition from Sacasa and backed former Conservative President Aldofo Díaz, who was elected chief executive by the Nicaraguan Congress in November 1926. This episode demonstrated again that U.S. interference in the republic's domestic conflicts had been detrimental to the aspirations of Liberal politicians. Forcing Chamorro out of office incurred the wrath of this popular figure who later would do his best to thwart a United States election project.

Recognition of Díaz did not end Sacasa's determination to claim his rightful post. He continued to fight the Conservative army and set up a provisional capital in Puerto Cabezas, on the Atlantic coast. Moreover, President Plutarco Elias Calles of Mexico recognized his government in December 1926. The United States, viewing Mexican meddling in Nicaragua's affairs as a real threat, increased its arms shipments to a marine contingent that had previously landed along the Nicaraguan east coast to protect North American lives and property. The United States was therefore prepared to support the Conservative party.[5] Yet the Coolidge Administration was not allowed to pursue this course without strong opposition at home. Through propaganda efforts, the Sacasa forces had been able to attract international attention in their campaign to restore constitutional government and win the support of a number of North American congressmen. President Calvin Coolidge faced a skeptical Senate and House of Representatives whose members questioned the United States' role in Nicaragua's domestic embroilment. Congress would not accept U.S. strategy for a direct role in Managua's politics for the sake of preserving peace and stability without some explanation.

In early January, President Coolidge lifted the embargo he had briefly placed on both sides in the Conservative/Liberal civil war and allowed arms shipments to be sent only to the Conservative forces. This action provoked a response in the United States House of Representatives and even from some of the more powerful voices in the Senate, including Senator William Borah of Idaho, chairman of the Foreign Relations Committee. The senator had been a long-time critic of Republican leadership in foreign affairs. He looked with misgivings on the Coolidge Administration's plan for supporting President Díaz and thereby becoming directly involved in a foreign civil

---

[5] *Congressional Record*, 69th Cong., 2d sess., January 11, 1927, 1428.

war.[6] Although Borah supported Sacasa's claim to the presidency, he centered his argument on the need for maintaining and upholding the idea of legitimacy as a beginning for establishing responsible government in Nicaragua.

Opposition to the Coolidge policy supporting Díaz also gathered momentum in the House of Representatives.[7] In numerous speeches, members raised questions as to the exact reason and purpose for the presence of marines in Nicaragua and why some explanation had not been forthcoming from the State Department on the subject.[8] Secretary of State Frank Kellogg had not made any effort to justify publicly the United States embargo action.

Senator Burton Wheeler of Montana also joined the administration's critics. As a follow-up to Borah's call for withdrawal of the marines, Wheeler suggested that Vice-President Sacasa be allowed to succeed to the presidency. The Montana senator then introduced a resolution on January 4, 1927, which stated it was the "sense of the Senate that U.S. marines should be removed from Nicaraguan soil, warships should be withdrawn immediately from all ports in that country, and Sacasa should be recognized as successor to President Carlos Solórzano," the coalition president whom Chamorro had forced to resign. The resolution also stated that Díaz did not legally occupy the chief executive's chair.

A direct challenge had been aimed at the administration's policy in Nicaragua. Coolidge responded to Senate and House speeches in a message to Congress on January 10 and with Secretary of State Kellogg's testimony before a Senate Foreign Relations Committee secret session. The president was frank in his explanations for U.S. involvement in the Nicaraguan embroilment. First, he said the opposition to Díaz was aggravated by Mexico's recognition and support for the Liberal Sacasa. The president insisted the interference of this southern neighbor in Central America clearly jeopardized present and

---

6 Ibid., 1444-1445.

7 Ibid., January 10, 1927, 1324.

8 Ibid., 1326. Secretary Kellogg appeared before a U.S. Senate Foreign Relations Committee secret session on January 12, 1927. *The New York Times*, January 13, 1927. Public attention may have been drawn to U.S. involvement in Nicaragua and Mexico's competing interests there in this article: Carlton Beals, "Mexico Seeking Central American Leadership," *Current History* 24 (September 1926): 839-844.

future canal rights and investments in the area. In his report, the chief executive also noted the United States' "particular responsibility" in Nicaragua and concern over a threat to its stability caused by a civil war. This, he emphasized, could bring about the active interests of "outside forces." He was, of course, referring directly to the assistance Sacasa was receiving from Mexico.[9] Coolidge's message and Kellogg's testimony did not satisfy opponents of United States intervention in Nicaraguan politics. The president's statement affirmed the difficulties accompanying intervention and tried to justify the presence of marines in the Nicaraguan capital as a need to preserve economic and strategic interests.

　　Senator William Borah (R-Idaho and Chair, Foreign Relations Committee) took the initiative and suggested that members of the Foreign Relations Committee visit Nicaragua on a fact-finding mission to ascertain the causes for the civil war and try to affix blame. His proposal for a congressional inquiry into the Nicaraguan problems was clearly a direct challenge to the Coolidge administration's management of foreign policy in Central America, and some response by the executive branch seemed necessary.

---

[9] Beals said that Mexico's close cultural ties with Central America made it a natural ally in the face of a North American threat. The Coolidge administration also saw similarities in the Mexican and Russian revolutions and equated Mexican assistance to Sacasa with the spread of Bolshevism in Nicaragua. See James J. Horn, "United States Diplomacy and the Specter of Bolshevism in Mexico," *Americas* 32 (July 1975): 31-32.

II

Supervised Elections: Henry L. Stimson — Eyes, Ears, and More

UNDER THE PRODDING OF numerous congressional speeches and the danger of losing the initiative in conducting foreign affairs in Central America to a Senate committee, President Coolidge decided to bring the Nicaraguan conflict into sharper perspective and ascertain for himself and his administration the facts surrounding the conflict. The chief executive was faced with two choices. One, let the Díaz government fall to a Mexican-backed, Liberal Sacasa force or look for a negotiated settlement of the civil war. He called upon Henry L. Stimson, former secretary of war in the Taft Administration (1911-1913), for assistance in the Nicaraguan problem. The selection of this New York lawyer gave prominence to the Nicaraguan matter and Coolidge's effort to learn the facts from a competent, trusted public servant firsthand. Stimson's 40-year public career stretched from the Theodore Roosevelt administration to Harry Truman's, serving as the latter's secretary of war (Spring-December 1943).

Stimson realized the task would not be easy, mainly because of public controversy over United States involvement in Nicaraguan affairs. For example, he recorded in his diary that Coolidge had considerable difficulty finding an emissary for the assignment. He noted the president was reluctant "to trouble me again" and further quoted the chief executive as saying, "but if you cannot go, I really don't know who [sic] I can select for the mission."[1] Apparently on the further recommendation and prodding of Elihu Root, former secretary of war (1899-1904) and secretary of state (1903-1909), and Leonard

---

[1] Henry L. Stimson, Diary entry, April 1, 1927, Yale University Library, (New Haven, Conn.: Yale University).

Wood, then governor general of the Philippines (1921-1927), he was persuaded to accept the assignment.

Stimson's selection was clearly Coolidge's personal choice. Nothing indicates that Secretary of State Kellogg had any interest or influence in this appointment. Certainly Congress did not. The secretary of state was relieved to learn the Nicaraguan problem might be lifted from his direct responsibility, particularly at a time when Mexico's support for Sacasa was increasing and making the entire issue more difficult and dangerous to handle.[2]

Actually, this was not the first time Coolidge had called upon the former secretary of war for assistance in a complicated international matter. Stimson's advice was sought earlier in 1926 on a solution to the protracted and difficult Tacna-Arica dispute between Chile and Peru growing out of the War of the Pacific (1879-1882). Central to that conflict was the Chilean government's hold on the administrative machinery for conducting a plebiscite in the two territories. Most likely, the Chilean government would win the election and legally annex both areas. Stimson was convinced Coolidge was in an extremely difficult position on this issue as the United States might have to continue to recognize a government which conducted election procedures fraudulently, or by rejecting the result, give affront to a friendly country.[3]

Stimson's conclusions in his study of the Tacna-Arica problem were extremely significant in the manner in which he viewed the Nicaraguan crisis. In his report to the State Department in 1926, he noted that a fair election in the disputed Tacna-Arica area could not be a free one where "one of the contestants is in control of the civil machinery."[4] Essentially, Stimson viewed the Chilean-Peruvian plebiscite as a potentially different situation, where U.S. election supervision did not have enough power to control voting procedures. Consequently, the purely advisory duties in a plebiscite of General John J. Pershing and his successor General William Lassiter were ineffective in securing a genuinely free and fair vote, in

---

[2] L. Ethan Ellis, *Frank B. Kellogg and American Foreign Relations, 1925-1939* (New Brunswick: Rutgers University Press, 1961), 72.

[3] Stimson, Diary entry, May 1, 1926.

[4] Ibid., entry May 28, 1926.

Stimson's opinion.[5] As a result, his conclusions in the Tacna-Arica dispute called for taking the election machinery entirely out of the hands of Chile and Peru and placing election supervision in the exclusive care of the United States.[6]

Convinced that the Nicaraguan situation was similar to the earlier Chilean-Peruvian dispute, Stimson considered the possibility of making an arrangement with the incumbent Conservative government to have the United States run a presidential election and avoid the embarrassment which he referred to in 1926, namely facing the prospect of recognizing a regime which might succeed itself at the polls by fraud. Moreover, Coolidge's personal emissary envisioned a new approach toward intervention projects in Central America, which primarily meant allowing an incumbent regime to stay in power, arranging a truce between warring parties, and supervising elections.

As Stimson prepared to leave for his Nicaraguan assignment, Robert Olds, assistant secretary of state, prepared a definitive statement concerning United States policy in Central America and Nicaragua in particular. The memorandum set forth a policy framework around which Stimson contemplated a unique strategy for a United States-run election while allowing elected officials to retain their positions.[7] The policy paper said in part:

> If any country can ever be held to have a special interest in a given area, it is the United States in its relation to all of Central America lying south of the Republic of Mexico. Until now the world at large has at least tacitly conceded this position.[8]

Since the perceived challenge to United States hegemony in Central America came in large part from Mexico, Olds concluded from this:

---

[5] Ibid.

[6] Henry L. Stimson and McGeorge Bundy, *On Active Service in Peace and War* (New York: Harper and Brothers, 1948), 110.

[7] Robert Olds, *Memorandum on Nicaragua*, January 1927, Department of State, Record Group 59, Decimal File 817.00/5854, National Archives (hereafter cited as *RG, DF, NA*).

[8] Ibid.

> The evidence now at hand indicates pretty clearly
> that unless we are willing to go beyond measures
> appropriate for the mere protection of [North]
> American lives and property in the affected terri-
> tory, there will be considerable bloodshed, and the
> government we have recognized will be driven
> from power. This means that the Sacasa govern-
> ment, which we have refused to recognize, will take
> charge with the backing of Mexico.[9]

Outcries in Congress against intervention again by the
marines seemed to carry little weight with the assistant
secretary. In fact, he thought the question of whether the
United States executive had the power to intervene, as had
been raised by members of Congress, was inconsequential.
However, he did recognize the need to present the legislative
branch with some plan for direct action in Nicaragua but
thought the time had not come for "so bold an act of
statesmanship."[10]

Stimson's mission was announced to be primarily fact-
gathering for the president. His diary reveals this was not the
case. The president had clarified his position when Stimson
asked if his duty was to be "your eyes and ears and make a
report, nothing more." Coolidge promptly replied, "I want you
to go somewhat further. If you find a chance to straighten the
matter out, I want you to do so."[11]

The president was anxious to end the civil war, yet he was
not prepared to adopt Olds' suggestion of an all-out military
invasion even though a contingent of marines had been sent
into the country to protect North American lives and property.
Coolidge decided to provide Stimson with considerable power
for ending the strife diplomatically.

The conferences held at the White House with Stimson
and Olds did not spell out the exact objectives of the special
mission. The president was willing, however, to give Stimson
considerable authority to decide what action to take once his

---

9 Ibid.

10 Ibid.

11 Stimson, Diary entry, April 1, 1927. See also William Kamman,
*A Search for Stability: United States Diplomacy toward Nicaragua
1925-1933* (South Bend: University of Notre Dame Press, 1968), 97.

special envoy reached Central America. Therefore, no formal instructions were drawn up. Clearly, President Coolidge had no definitive plan for ending the civil war. This lack of specificity left Stimson puzzled but confident he had considerable leverage for negotiation.[12] He understood that he was authorized to arrange for the end of hostilities and to bring both the Díaz and Sacasa forces to the peace table. All this was to be accomplished without a direct full-scale military intervention or takeover of the Nicaraguan government.

Faced with the task of ending a war, Stimson set down his thoughts for a solution in early April 1927, shortly after his conference with Coolidge. First and foremost, he thought that the United States had to set the terms of an armistice.[13] He was also prepared to insist that Adolfo Díaz be retained as the Nicaraguan president.[14] The question of the incumbent's right to hold office was not to be discussed, for this would only add to the already long list of problems to be solved. Stimson thought if the United States consented to removing Díaz as a means to conclude a Liberal/Conservative settlement, they would acknowledge the doubtful legality of the incumbent's tenure.

Stimson's plan to retain Díaz in office meant, of course, denying Sacasa's claim to the presidency. He was prepared to use force if necessary to prevent the Liberal leader from coming to power. Coolidge agreed with Stimson's views but offered no suggestions as to how to accomplish this goal. This was to be his envoy's unique, special task.

Coolidge's emissary considered the idea of having the United States supervise an election as a means to allow the Liberal forces a reasonable chance to elect a president. If Sacasa agreed to surrender his arms, Stimson planned to promise him and his party a free election without fraud and intimidation. His formula for peace in Nicaragua was therefore to be in the form of a "threat/promise scheme."[15]

Neither Secretary of State Kellogg nor President Coolidge

[12] Henry L. Stimson to Frank R. McCoy, April 8, 1927, "General correspondence 1925-1927," Frank McCoy Papers, File Box 18, Manuscript Division, Library of Congress.

[13] Memorandum, Stimson, April 4, 1927, *Official Papers of the Public Career of Henry L. Stimson*, Yale University Library.

[14] Ibid.

[15] Stimson, Diary entry, April 3, 1927.

had specific recommendations for implementing a supervised election. This, together with their noncommittal statements on how to secure peace, convinced Stimson his scope of authority was unlimited and his idea of a supervised election was a potentially good method for solving the political crisis. However, his independence left him somewhat apprehensive of success without policy direction from either the State Department or the White House.[16]

Soon after Stimson's assignment was announced, two figures began working on behalf of Chamorro's candidacy for Nicaragua's presidency. The first was an attorney, Chandler P. Anderson, a former State Department special counsel (1910-1913) and legal adviser to the Nicaraguan legation when Chamorro was minister in the United States. Second was Alejandro César, the Nicaraguan envoy in Washington. They were to be Chamorro's eyes and ears in the United States. While Kellogg and Olds were considering steps to quiet the uproar in Congress, Anderson urged them to adopt what he thought to be the simplest solution, which was to reject both Sacasa and Díaz.[17] Olds turned down this idea although there is some indication he thought it was good. Olds feared Chamorro would reappear and remain president without regard to any limitation on the length of his term.[18]

Not content just to plead his case before the State Department, Anderson met with Stimson just before the latter left for Nicaragua. Anderson forcefully presented his case on behalf of Chamorro and urged that no precipitous steps be taken to antagonize his client. He further warned that if Chamorro were excluded from Stimson's discussions with other Nicaraguan party leaders, the former president might decide to obstruct plans for a United States-supervised election. Anderson said this could be done because the Conservative party machinery was firmly controlled by the Chamorrista faction and not by President Díaz. These were indeed wise and prophetic words as time was to show.[19] Stimson, however, told Anderson that his mission was solely designed to secure

---

16 Stimson to McCoy, April 8, 1927, McCoy Papers.

17 Chandler P. Anderson, Diary, March 31, 1927, Manuscripts Division, File Box 7, Library of Congress.

18 Ibid.

19 Ibid., April 7, 1927.

information for Coolidge on the current conditions in the war and prospects for peace.[20]

Convinced, and correctly so, the United States government did not have a firmly established policy for Stimson to follow, Anderson started his campaign to launch Chamorro's drive for the presidency. He was assisted by Alejandro César, the Nicaraguan minister, who urged Chamorro to come to the United States from his "exile post" as minister to France and plead his case before the Department of State.[21]

Enter Stimson

While César and Anderson were preparing for Chamorro's return to Washington, Stimson sailed from New York aboard the Chilean steamship *Aconcagua* on April 9. Crossing the Isthmus of Panama and sailing on the United States cruiser *Trenton* from Panama City to Nicaragua's west coast port of Corinto, he reached Managua on the 17th of the same month. While traveling from the Pacific port city of Corinto to Managua, he became aware of the chaotic situation in the country, especially the damage done to many towns during the civil war. He was particularly disturbed by the intense bitterness displayed by both sides. The age-old hatred between the Liberal and Conservative parties could be felt, as he said, even in the "neutral city of Managua."[22]

Charles Eberhardt, the United States minister, reported to the president's emissary that José Maria Moncada, Sacasa's minister of war and commander of the Constitutionalist army, would not accept Díaz as president under any circumstances. Above all, he would not recognize him as a condition in agreeing to a supervised election. Stimson concluded that the State Department's intelligence reports on the civil war had been grossly inaccurate. Moncada's forces were large in number and commanded by competent leaders who controlled well over half the terrain outside the zones the United States had declared as neutral. Moreover, while the Díaz forces were larger, their leadership bordered on incompetence.

---

[20] Ibid.

[21] Ibid., May 2, 1927.

[22] Henry L. Stimson, *American Policy in Nicaragua* (New York: Charles Scribner's Sons, 1927), 46.

Stimson reasoned it would probably be difficult to deal with the Liberal general, an excellent military strategist who was well aware of his tactical successes, and more troublesome, he refused to recognize Díaz.[23]

Rather than confront General Moncada directly and impose his project, Stimson went about the business of securing the president's recognition through a person he thought might prove more acceptable to the Liberals, namely Carlos Cuadra Pasos, a prominent lawyer and foreign minister under Díaz. On him Stimson based his hopes and chances for persuading the combatants to cease fighting. Evidently, Cuadra Pasos was neither the chief strategist in the Díaz camp nor as intractable as many of Chamorro's followers.

Stimson raised the prospect of a United States-run election at his meeting with Carlos Cuadra Pasos in April 1927. Coolidge's emissary explained frankly that the United States traditionally had sought peace and stability in Central America and the Caribbean by merely indicating support of one regime or another or by using military force to occupy and govern a state. Stimson suggested that to create public confidence and governmental responsibility now, a structure providing for honest elections, leaving Díaz in power and guaranteeing an orderly succession of presidential leadership through supervised elections, could be established to prevent fraud by the incumbent regime. Cuadra Pasos appeared willing to accept the idea although Stimson wrote in his diary the foreign minister was not enthusiastic about it.[24]

Stimson promptly took advantage of Cuadra Pasos' guarded interest and pushed his plan even further by urging a U.S.-supervised election with full supervisory powers and emphasizing details of the plan to be worked out later. Cuadra Pasos agreed, confidently asserting that ultimately his party would have a great deal to say in drawing up the election laws.

Stimson stated bluntly that all members of the Liberal party had to consent to the supervision as well. Above all, both groups were to ask officially for a United States-supervised

---

[23] Stimson, Diary entry, April 17, 1927. In an effort to ameliorate differences, President Díaz had suggested that Liberals be named to judicial positions and allow them to hold congressional elections without opposition in areas where the civil war had disrupted the peace. Some Liberals proposed that the presidency go to someone outside the traditional parties.

[24] Ibid., Diary entry, April 18, 1927.

election, this to be a demonstration of cooperation and willingness to make peace.[25]

Cuadra Pasos proved to be helpful in most respects. He frequently reminded Stimson, however, that the incumbent Conservative regime risked losing in a supervised contest.[26]

Stimson's contacts and discussions with the Sacasa Liberals were to be a more difficult experience. Dr. Enoc Aguado, a noted lawyer and widely respected member of the Liberal party, was considered by the North American legation as the best contact in the effort to persuade the Sacasa group to make peace. Aguado enthusiastically endorsed the idea of a United States-supervised election but strongly objected to Stimson's recommendation that President Díaz be allowed to remain in office. He was convinced, as was the Liberal party leadership shortly thereafter, the only way to insure fairness in the 1928 presidential race was to eradicate all attempts at fraud and intimidation used by the incumbent party office holders. Aguado had supported the idea for creating an independent, nonpartisan native constabulary commanded by United States personnel as the country's sole police force. The suggestion for a National Guard was not originally proposed in this Stimson/ Aguado conference. It had been considered previously during the Solórzano/Sacasa administration (1924-1926).[27]

Stimson carefully exercised the independence granted him by the North American president as he proceeded in his difficult negotiations with the Liberals. Within a short time he was surprised to learn, in the form of rather vague instructions, that the State Department did not want him "to act as mediator in the civil war but only to make such arrangements as to have both sides seek his advice and counsel." Stimson thought this rather ambiguous direction indicated a lack of clarity and purpose that characterized most of the State Department's actions up to this time in the Nicaraguan matter.

It is true, of course, President Coolidge had asked Stimson only for a report, but he also encouraged Stimson's efforts to stop the civil war. However, Stimson's plan for a supervised election was at first not fully acceptable to Secretary of State Kellogg. Nevertheless, the president's emissary proceeded to implement the necessary steps to have both the Liberal and Conservative parties agree to a peace settlement.[28] Sensing

---

[25] Ibid.

[26] Ibid., Diary entry, April 18, 1927.

State Department procrastination and indecisiveness, he decided to use his own judgment and to proceed alone without specific instructions to work for a supervised election agreement. However, he vigorously expressed his opinion to the State Department that the tradition of government-controlled elections in Nicaragua meant continued rule which only a coup d'état could end.[29]

Stimson proceeded to plan for what he called "constructive intervention which would lead the country nearer to self government." This meant a significant departure from some United States intervention projects of the past, namely allowing a government to remain intact. The United States legation in Managua was completely in accord with his plans for a closely supervised election. Moreover, after conferring with the British chargé, who said England would follow the United States lead in its efforts for pacification, Stimson appeared more confident than ever that he was doing the right thing for U.S. interests. He then moved to secure the acceptance of his plan from as many government and opposition leaders as possible.[30]

It is not clear whether Stimson had any thoughts for enlarged U.S. control of Nicaragua's finances as a means to prevent fraud and misuse of government funds during a presidential election. However, his interview with Minister of Finance Antonio Gúzman, in whom he had little confidence, might be considered as an exploratory meeting leading to further direct control of Nicaragua's fiscal policies. Gúzman saw the futility in opposing the wishes of the U.S. government and readily accepted the idea of an election under U.S. supervision. He even went so far as to suggest that presidential candidates and all cabinet appointments be officially approved by the State Department.[31] Despite the encouraging meeting with Gúzman, Stimson was not convinced of the Díaz government's unqualified acceptance of his supervised election plans.

Having secured the tacit approval of some of Díaz's important ministers and confident of Coolidge's implicit sup-

---

[28] Ibid., Diary entry, April 16, 1927. Assistant Secretary of State Joseph C. Grew to U.S. legation, Nicaragua, April 15, 1927, Photocopied.

[29] Ibid.

[30] Ibid., Diary entry, April 19, 1927.

[31] Ibid.

port, Stimson decided to place Washington on record supporting election supervision. By April, he still had not received State
Department approval for implementing his formula for ending
the civil war. But he could wait no longer; so, without formal
authorization, he obtained a verbal agreement from President
Díaz and Nicaraguan Foreign Minister Carlos Cuadra Pasos.
The Conservative government accepted Stimson's proposals:
allowing Díaz to stay in office until after the election; filling out
his term; granting amnesty to all combatants; appointing
Liberals in government positions; and abolishing the old
constabulary. A new one would be created and run by the
United States.[32]

Having obtained an agreement from Conservative leaders, Stimson now planned his strategy to secure the same
agreement from the Liberals. This was to prove far more
difficult. To begin with, Sacasa's government operated from the
Atlantic coast city of Puerto Cabezas, and contact with it would
be difficult. To complicate matters, the State Department grew
disturbed over Stimson's newly publicized role and again
reminded him not to mediate between the two forces — only
make sure the combatants sought his advice.

Nevertheless, he proceeded to contact Gustavo Argüello,
a prominent Liberal and Sacasa's minister of government, who
the United States thought was willing to accept Stimson's peace
proposals. More importantly, he anticipated this Liberal could
act as a contact man with the east coast Sacasa government.
Coolidge's emissary asked Argüello to inform the Liberal leader
of the United States' peace plan. Specifically, he was asked to
present the same proposals to Sacasa but adding that all arms
be turned over to United States forces and accepting U.S.
supervision of the 1928 election.[33]

Contents of Stimson's proposal were sent to Sacasa. He
was persuaded to send delegates to Managua to meet with the

---

[32] Ibid. President Díaz had already proposed publicly that the
United States supervise the 1928 election. *The New York Times*,
January 16, 1927, 1. In February 1927, he suggested that a Nicaraguan
Platt Amendment in a Nicaragua/United States Treaty of Alliance be
agreed upon whereby Nicaragua would "pledge not to contract
financial obligations without consent of the [North] American government, nor would the country sell or lease territory or perform any act
which would impair its independence." Kamman, *Search for Stability*, 94.

[33] Stimson, Diary entry, April 19, 1927.

U.S. emissary. Because Coolidge's "special envoy" suggested a U.S.-supervised election, Sacasa was convinced that talks with the North American in the nation's capital could be fruitful although many of his followers were reluctant to allow Díaz to continue in office.

The conferences began on April 30 in Tipitapa, 15 miles from Managua and strategically near the advancing army led by Moncada. The Sacasa delegates found Stimson frank and open in his discussions and soon learned the United States trouble-shooter was firm in his decision to continue support of Díaz as president. Stimson stated bluntly that the proposed supervised election offered two choices for the Sacasa forces. First, assuming of course that Sacasa accepted Díaz leadership, the North American-run election would give the Liberal leader a fair chance to win the presidency along with United States diplomatic recognition. Second, the Liberals might continue the conflict but with no chance of recognition even if they secured the presidency and gained control of the nation militarily. This dire warning was not overlooked by the Sacasa representatives.[34]

In the concluding moments of the first meeting with the Liberal emissaries, Stimson presented them with a veiled threat by stating the Conservatives were now willing to accept his proposals for peace. He referred to a report being drafted to President Coolidge conveying a lack of cooperation on the part of the Liberals. This would, in his words, "create a very unfavorable impression in the United States." [35]

Satisfied he had been forceful enough without threatening direct intervention, Stimson informed the Sacasa delegation that Díaz had enthusiastically agreed to the proposals. This was not entirely true as the president had not yet made a firm, unqualified promise to cooperate with the United States. Carlos Cuadra Pasos was the only government official who had agreed — and only verbally at that — to Stimson's proposals.[36]

The Department of State finally accepted Stimson's suggestion for a supervised election in an effort to end the Nicaraguan civil war. Relieved and emboldened, Stimson decided to continue talks with the Liberals and, at the same

---

[34] Ibid., Diary entry, April 30, 1927, confidential telegram from Secretary of State Kellogg to Stimson, Photocopy.

[35] Ibid.

[36] Ibid.

time, disarm the Liberal army forcibly if they persisted in not recognizing the Díaz government.[37] Liberal delegation members first wanted to meet with General Moncada before finalizing an agreement. Stimson was also anxious to speak personally with the military leader.[38]

Stimson had informed Secretary of State Kellogg of the Liberal opposition to Díaz which, in Stimson's view, had prevented a final solution to the civil war. Clearly, the Díaz issue was the only hindrance in concluding final peace. So adamant did the Liberal delegates appear in refusing to recognize the president, and so determined had the State Department become to reach a peaceful solution to the conflict, the United States briefly considered a plan to support the ouster of Díaz in an effort to appease the Sacasa forces and end the war.[39]

Stimson was not at all pleased with the prospect of removing Díaz. He was convinced the president was the kind of person who would be "a mere figurehead as far as executive power is concerned." Therefore, on Stimson's advice, the proposal for ousting Díaz was summarily dropped.[40] Yet Coolidge's representative seriously considered the possibility of selecting a United States citizen to be the provisional executive chief should Díaz actually be forced by the Liberals to step aside. On reflection, however, he thought this might involve complicated legal and constitutional questions, so he abandoned the idea. Stimson was determined to see Díaz remain in office and was willing to use military force if necessary to accomplish this. The warning had already been delivered to the Liberal delegates who were holding out for an agreement. They based their hopes on an aroused world opinion which would force the United States to retreat from its announced determination to keep the Conservative president in office.[41]

Having delivered a virtual ultimatum to the Sacasa delegates, Stimson embarked on a plan to bring the commander

---

[37] Ibid., Diary entry, April 23, 1927.

[38] Kamman, *Search for Stability*, 106-7.

[39] Stimson, Diary entry, April 30, 1927; telegram, Department of State to Stimson, Photocopy.

[40] Ibid., Diary entry, May 2, 1927.

[41] Ibid.

of the Liberal forces to the peace table. He thought if the head of the Liberal army could be persuaded to make peace, Sacasa's intransigence could be overcome easily. General Moncada meanwhile hesitated to meet Stimson mainly because his subordinates feared, and with some justification as will be seen, the United States was about to disarm his army forcibly.[42]

In May, Stimson advised General Moncada to accept Díaz and cease his military operations or else the United States would move to disarm his troops.[43] After a short conference with Sacasa's delegates that same day, the Liberal military commander decided not to resist. Moncada therefore issued the necessary orders for his troops to disarm.[44] Stimson again emphasized the need for recognizing Díaz and keeping him in office. Moncada clearly saw the U.S. emissary's determination and agreed to the provisions Stimson had drawn up for peace between the two parties. They were: immediate and general peace in time for harvesting of a new crop and both parties' simultaneous delivery of arms to North American custody; general amnesty and return of exiles and confiscated property; appointment of Liberals to the Díaz cabinet; the nonpartisan organization of a constabulary, commanded by U.S. military officers; U.S.-supervised 1928 elections; and the U.S. Marines to remain in the country, enforcing the foregoing provisions.[45]

General Moncada suggested the Liberal party hold a plebiscite to see if party members would support a United States-supervised election. He made this proposal fearing he would be criticized for being too pliable in surrendering military gains made by his forces in the war. Actually, some of his chief lieutenants were already accusing him of relinquishing his strong position both militarily and politically by meeting

---

[42] José M. Moncada, *Estados Unidos en Nicaragua* (Managua: Tipgrafia Tenas, 1942), 2.

[43] Stimson, Diary entry, May 4, 1927.

[44] Ibid.

[45] Stimson, *American Policy*, 63-64. See also Stimson, Diary, memorandum, Stimson, Eberhardt, Latimer, and Moncada, May 5, 1927. Earlier, President Díaz had proposed as a solution to the national crisis that he be allowed to finish his term and that Liberals be named to executive and judicial posts and elected to Congress without opposition in areas where revolutionary activity had earlier disrupted election procedures. Among other proposals, Díaz suggested a United States-run 1928 election. For details on these proposals, see Kamman, *Search for Stability*, 89-90.

with the North American representative.

Sacasa vehemently rejected Stimson's tactics at Tipitapa. On May 4 he sent a letter of protest to his representatives at the meeting and castigated the United States government for nullifying the inherent right of a Central American state to oust a regime which came to power as the result of a coup d'état and which, in his words, "smashed not only the constitution of the Republic but also the Central American Treaty signed in Washington...." [Signed in 1923, the treaty forced Isthmian governments to recognize any regime seizing power, even by coup d'état.][46]

Consolidation of Intervention:
Control of the National Election Board

Even though General Moncada and the Sacasa delegates finally, though reluctantly, signed an agreement for peace with the Díaz government, many Liberals were still unhappy. They did not object to the provision which made them accept U.S. supervision of the forthcoming presidential election, but disliked the point calling for the continued recognition of Díaz. Stimson, however, was determined to retain him and launch his electoral supervision project in 1928.[47] His approach in this intervention project was to leave a government in power, arrange a truce in a civil war as done earlier in Haiti, the Dominican Republic, and Cuba, then gradually withdraw military forces when a "nonpartisan army" could be trained. But this policy differed from earlier interventions in these Caribbean States, which were implemented largely for the protection of United States property and establishing a military government during an extended period of time.

As a first step in the preparation for U.S. supervision, Stimson insisted changes begin in the Nicaraguan supreme court where the selection of an electoral chairman would be made. He informed Díaz that the Chamorro-appointed justices would have to be removed, fearing they would undertake disruptive tactics as a protest to United States treatment of the former president.[48] President Díaz carried out the demand and promptly removed three justices. Stimson took note of the speed with which the president had acted and was gratified

[46] Stimson, Diary entry, May 5, 1927. Letter from Juan Bautista Sacasa to his representatives at Tipitapa, Photocopy.

[47] Ibid., May 7, 1927. See also Eberhardt to Department of State, May 12, 1927, RG 59, DF 817.00/4775, NA.

[48] Stimson, Diary entry, May 6, 1927.

over what he called "the vindication of an independent judiciary."[49]

The successful removal of the Chamorro appointees eliminated a potential obstacle of appointing a supervisor for the 1928 election. The court purge was significant because Stimson wanted to show the Liberals that the United States was planning to take an active role in the coming election and would not tolerate interference from any sector of the incumbent Conservative regime. Stimson noted in his diary on more than one occasion during the peace negotiations that Sacasa's emissaries had referred to previous cases where the United States asked Liberals to agree to an election only to learn the North American republic had decided to support the incumbent Conservative party's candidate.[50]

The Liberals had been only partially satisfied to learn Chamorro's appointed judges had been purged. Now they insisted that representatives from their party be placed on election boards in every department in which they had achieved a majority in the 1924 election. Consequently, Stimson and the United States legation asked the Díaz government to make the proper changes based on the Liberals' request. In two days, Carlos Cuadra Pasos reported new appointments had been made to the satisfaction of the Liberal party. In sum, Stimson was having little trouble directing the chief executive's actions in response to Sacasa's demands to test his diplomatic skill and influence.

The appointment of Liberal representatives to election boards in departments where they had a majority of registered voters marked a turning point in the early stages of the 1928 supervised presidential election. It indicated Stimson's determination to show the Conservatives that they were not to enjoy an unchallenged position in the pre-election activities as they had in the past. More significant, the Liberals were less skeptical now of Stimson's promise for impartial election supervision.

By early May, Coolidge's emissary had completed his plan for the 1928 contest independently of State Department directives. His first step was to have the United States president

---

[49] Ibid. Chamorro immediately saw the significance of this tactic and made preparations to confront it. Interview with author, April 17, 1965 (Managua).

[50] Ibid., Diary entry, May 1, 1927.

appoint a national election board chairman who would then be formally appointed by the Nicaraguan chief executive. Also, the United States would have to construct a new electoral law for the Nicaraguan Congress to pass.

Stimson proposed that the chairman of the national election board and heads of the 13 department boards throughout the country be United States citizens. Therefore, each board would have three members: a North American in charge; one representative each from the Liberal and Conservative parties. Stimson contemplated an election law which would give the United States chairman extensive powers to arbitrate any dispute and exercise a veto over any action by an electoral board at any level which was suspected of denying anyone the opportunity to vote.

In a conference with Carlos Cuadra Pasos in the first week of May, Stimson said he wanted the Nicaraguan army disbanded. He thought its past political activities posed a threat to a fair election. It was therefore suggested, not for the first time, that a non-political constabulary be established. Its ranks were to be filled with people conspicuous by their lack of participation in political affairs. With the hope of insuring the constabulary's impartiality, United States officers would command it. Cuadra Pasos was anything but enthusiastic about the creation of a constabulary. He did not believe it was possible to establish a non-political military unit as the project seemed to him to be unrealistic in light of the traditional role the army played in Nicaraguan politics.[51]

The foreign minister's feelings on this subject were supported initially by Assistant Secretary of Foreign Affairs José Barcenas. Cuadra Pasos' subordinate later agreed, however, to the formation of a new constabulary on the condition the United States army take charge and not the marines.[52] Stimson immediately rejected this suggestion because the marine contingent was already in the country and would remain to assist in the presidential election. Cuadra Pasos then agreed to send Stimson's suggestions for 1928 election supervision to the Nicaraguan minister in the United States, who in turn would

---

[51] Carlos Cuadra Pasos, "Introdución a la Historia de la Guardia Nacional." *Revista Conservadora del Pensamiento Centroamericano* (August 1961): 6.

[52] Ibid.

submit them in the form of a formal request to the U.S. government.[53]

While the Díaz regime and the United States moved toward an election supervision plan, the Chamorro wing of the Conservative party remained totally excluded from the deliberations surrounding Stimson's mission — a near fatal mistake later when the United States tried to have its election law legally approved by the Nicaraguan Congress. Coolidge's emissary had been warned earlier, if the former president were ignored in the negotiation process, he might decide to hinder the United States' subsequent efforts to run a presidential contest. Chamorro, in fact, exerted considerable pressure on Díaz, forcing him to act more independently in his talks with Stimson. President Díaz, weary of the constant harassments from the Chamorro wing of his party, suddenly decided to resign in the spring. He thought this move would either eliminate the possibility of a party split and thereby improve its chances for a 1928 election victory or, more likely, force the United States to reiterate its support for him.

In any case, the disastrous consequences of such an action were clear to Stimson. The only real unqualified cooperation he had received in Nicaragua was now about to succumb to the pressures of a disruptive but powerful element in the Nicaraguan Congress led by the Chamorrista wing of the Conservative party. This crisis, of course, had to be dealt with immediately. On May 12, United States Minister Charles Eberhardt and Stimson met Díaz. Much to their concern, they found him thoroughly disgusted and disturbed by frequent challenges to his leadership by Conservative party leaders who questioned a continued United States presence in the country. Both North Americans urged him to remain firm towards his own partisans and Liberals. Eberhardt and Stimson promised if he did, the United States would guarantee his position.[54] Undoubtedly worried and looking for an issue to make the president change his mind, they appealed to his patriotism and stressed the importance of his role at this time of civil strife. The North American diplomats pointed out that Díaz was the only man who could guarantee Nicaragua a free and fair election in 1928 by his willingness to remain in office. Obviously, Díaz was flattered and felt strengthened politically and reassured by the attention given him. He thereupon withdrew his resignation

---

53 Stimson, Diary entry, May 9, 1927

54 Ibid., Diary entry, May 12, 1927.

threats, which obviously worked, and remained in office with unqualified U.S. support.[55]

Stimson completed his mission in mid-May 1927. He was more convinced than ever the United States had to maintain an active role in Central America's domestic affairs. Internal Nicaraguan peace was an important ingredient in this overall objective. He also thought the Coolidge administration had a duty to develop a new approach in U.S. intervention, starting with Nicaragua, whereby political groups would accept administrative machinery for conducting a nation's elections and not rely exclusively on United States military actions as in other Caribbean countries.[56] Evidently satisfied that he had been able to bring the two warring political groups together, Stimson departed for the west coast port of Corinto.

Stimson accomplished his primary objective as both sides' armies accepted a peace settlement and the two major parties had agreed, however reluctantly, to allow the United States to supervise and run the 1928 presidential election. Although the constitutional forces were beginning to be dismantled and Sacasa had gone into exile, the peace was a tenuous one. Liberals would remain unconvinced for some time as to United States efficacy in dislodging the Conservative party from its powerful position as the incumbent party. Moreover, the Sacasa forces were deeply split. Many of his followers went to Mexico, and others joined Liberal rebel Augusto César Sandino, a vehement anti-Yankee who pledged a campaign to end United States military intervention. Others joined Moncada and placed their hopes in a free and impartially-run election, a process which they thought would likely bring about a Liberal victory.

The armed forces of both political parties initially refused to surrender arms when Stimson asked them to, although the Conservatives were eager to comply since they were losing the war. In return for bringing the Liberals to the peace table, Stimson had forced the hand of President Díaz, whom he considered weak, pliable, and indecisive. In this manner he obtained the chief executive's consent for U.S. control of the 1928 presidential election. In June 1927, a significant number of leaders in both parties had accepted the inevitable, namely a dominant role for the United States in the nation's internal

---

[55] Ibid.

[56] Ibid., Diary entry May 16, 1927. Speech before Law School, University of Granada, Nicaragua, May 15, 1927.

conflicts and specifically in their coming electoral contest.

A very important segment of the Conservative party had been ignored in these early deliberations for ending the civil war and preparing for a presidential election. As a member of the Chamber of Deputies, Emiliano Chamorro, probably the most effective organizer and leader of the Conservative party, became the chief spokesman for those who opposed a supervised election on legal grounds. Sandino, who flatly rejected the peace of Tipitapa, was to lead military opposition to the United States.[57] His campaign was on a collision course with the Roosevelt corollary of the Monroe Doctrine, still an important feature in United States foreign policy in the Caribbean and Central America. Stimson described his government's position, at least as he perceived it, regarding intervention in the internal affairs of Central American states:[58]

> The natural result of such a situation is that if we will not permit European nations to project their customary rights within this zone, we must, to a certain extent, make ourselves responsible for this protection. To a certain extent, at least, we must assume the attitude of seeing that [North] American countries within this zone fulfill their obligations as independent nations to the outside world.[59]

Therefore, Sandino prepared a strategy to end this policy. His chief objective as a nationalist was to force the withdrawal of the United States Marines and prevent election supervisors from administering political contests in Nicaragua. Both the Chamorrista and Sacasa forces objected to U.S. intervention and, for different reasons, supported Sandino — a man with no

---

[57] Considerable controversy surrounds Sandino's actions regarding the Tipitapa agreement. Some historians argue that the guerrilla leader agreed to disarm his forces and await Moncada's orders. Others say he would accept a direct military government, removing all Liberal and Conservative office holders, and run elections. See Neill Macaulay, *The Sandino Affair* (Durham, N.C.: Duke University Press, 1985), 65. Sandino's supporters claim that the rebel leader had no choice but to accept a surrender on Moncada's terms. See Kamman, *Search for Stability*, 121-22, and G. Aleman Bolaños, *¡Sandino!, Estudio Completo del Heroe de las Segovias* (Guatemala City: Imprenta La Republica, 1932), 16.

[58] Stimson, *American Policy*, 11.

[59] Ibid.

clear political or social ideology.

Sandino was born in 1895 in the small town of Niquinohomo, a village west of Granada. He was the natural son of Don Gregorio Sandino, a moderately wealthy land-owner, and Margarita Calderon, an Indian woman and servant in the family. One historian relates his brother's description of him as a "man of not robust constitution: five feet eight inches tall, very white complexion, black hair, and brown eyes. Sometimes he appeared in a coffee-colored hat with a sharp-pointed crown and broad brim, a red and black handkerchief around his neck, two pistols hanging from his belt with cartridge shells."[60]

After a brief stint administering his father's estate, he journeyed to Honduras and worked in United States-owned gold mines and in the banana plantations along the north coast. He then went to Tampico, Mexico, in 1923, where he worked in a subsidiary of the Southern Pennsylvania Oil Company, followed by the Huasteca Petroleum Enterprise run by Stan-dard Oil of Indiana. According to the same author, "...it was in Mexico that he began to think about [North] American domi-nation in Nicaragua and to form a social and political philoso-phy that Nicaragua's troubles lay in politicians and [North] American imperialism."[61] Tampico was a center of labor unrest and thriving radical politics.

Sandino returned to Nicaragua in 1924 and later in 1926 worked for the U.S.-owned San Albino mining company. He joined the Liberal revolt opposing Chamorro's coup d'état. He raised his own army and joined Sacasa and Moncada's consti-tutional government.

General José Maria Moncada's designation as the chief Liberal spokesman at the 1927 Tipitapa meeting gave every indication that Sacasa, claiming the right to succeed to the presidency, reposed confidence and trust in his military commander. Next to Sacasa, Moncada probably was one of the most popular, if not one of the more powerful figures in the Liberal party. Certainly his successful military campaign com-ing near to defeating the Conservative forces made him a likely choice as his party's representative at the Stimson conference.

As Sacasa's minister of war, Moncada's selection to be the spokesman for the Liberal cause placed him in a strong position politically. His designation as the Liberal leader's emissary was

---

[60] Kamman, *Search for Stability*, 123.

[61] Ibid.

a blow to Sandino, who hoped to maintain a degree of influence in the party's leadership. He had anticipated Moncada would include him in the negotiations as a gesture of confidence and respect for his successes against the Conservatives too. Rather than seek Sandino's advice on the many problems confronting the Liberal army, Moncada ordered him to disarm his troops, make peace with the Conservative forces, and accept a United States-supervised presidential election.

After the provisions of the Tipitapa conference were made known, Sandino continued a separate armed campaign and established his own military-political movement apart from the traditional Liberal and Conservative parties. He challenged Moncada's leadership, claiming he would "at the very first opportunity sell out to the [North] Americans; we must save the revolution from Moncada."[62]

When he organized his army, he proclaimed a war on Washington's military presence in his country. He refused to recognize Díaz and urged the destruction of all United States-owned property. Avoiding the appearance of social radicalism, he called for the union of his movement with the rest of Indo-Hispanic America. Haya de la Torre of Peru and Chilean poet Gabriela Mistral, among others, enthusiastically endorsed his efforts.

Anti-U.S. elements in Nicaragua and the rest of Latin America convinced Sandino he could grasp the reins of power in his party if he openly espoused the need for maintaining and preserving Nicaragua's political and territorial independence. Actually, the rebel leader considered his associations with members of the Liberal party rather awkward and thought he had never been part of the "sophisticated elements" surrounding Sacasa and Moncada.[63] He might well have been compared in some respects to Chamorro in the Conservative party. The intellectual and less demagogic elements supported Díaz and Carlos Cuadra Pasos, whereas Chamorro was more the practical and charismatic leader.

Sandino's innovative campaign, avoiding a conventional war and resorting to small-unit guerrilla force operations, was to be conducted primarily in the northern departments as well

---

[62] Manuel Antonio Valle, "Viva Sandino." *Living Age* 243 (November 1932): 63. See also Bolaños, *¡Sandino!*, 9. Neill Macaulay, *The Sandino Affair*, 63-64.

[63] Ibid.

as the northeastern sections of the country where United States economic interests were evident. His campaign also posed a threat to Moncada's leadership and to Stimson's plan for pacifying the country. Moncada used every opportunity to depict Sandino as a threat to the country's political stability and to the successful supervision of the 1928 election. He claimed the rebel was "fired by the desire to establish Bolshevism in Nicaragua."[64] This observation had some impact later on the chief of the United States electoral board as he oftentimes relayed this information to his associates in Managua and Washington. He urged his colleagues to be on the lookout for what he called a "cancerous philosophy which might spread to Nicaragua."[65] Moncada denounced Sandino also by warning the United States that the rebel wanted to govern the republic as a dictator.

Obviously aware North Americans were fearful of a Communist threat, Moncada asserted that Sandino was campaigning to establish a socialist state by "emulating Pancho Villa in military prowess."[66] In many respects, Moncada succeeded in convincing Washington that Sandino was as much a menace to it as he was to the two-party system and the upcoming 1928 elections.[67]

In the summer of 1928, as the supervision project began, it became clear the Sandino campaigns in the northern mountains and the country's east coast were effective. In fact, the national election board chairman admitted that the northern regions of the Segovia mountains and their poor communication with the rest of the republic gave Sandino's military campaign "a real possibility for success."[68] Later he emphasized that because the Díaz government had no means of controlling the northern areas, the rebel leader might overrun the entire region. U.S. diplomats in Managua, understating the problem, concluded Sandino had shown "unexpected strength" in his

---

[64] Memorandum — Sandino, n.d., Department of State, Records of the United States electoral mission to Nicaragua, 1928-1932, Records, 1928 mission RG 43, folder B-1, NA..

[65] General McCoy memorandum to department chairmen, April 18, 1928, Records, 1928 mission, RG 43, folder B-1, NA.

[66] Memorandum — Sandino.

[67] McCoy memorandum.

[68] Ibid.

guerrilla campaign, and marine efforts to subdue him would be difficult.[69]

As Stimson's mission ended, an insurgent rebel nationalist campaign began, which by 1928 had greatly commanded the attention and support of anti-imperialists both in Nicaragua and the rest of Latin America. Yet, Stimson was confident the Liberal General Moncada and President Díaz would keep their promises and carry out an election supervision plan. Coolidge's emissary believed the provisions for a United States-run election were sound because they helped to end a bloody and senseless civil war and avoided United States' direct rule over the country's affairs. In Stimson's view, his plan was a form of political education emphasizing an electoral process run by the country's political forces. He undoubtedly thought the United States would fulfill the commitments he had made personally to Moncada. However, Nicaragua's pledge was less complete as internal feuds within the nation's two political parties were overlooked in the peace settlement itself.

---

[69] *Washington Star,* May 13, 1928, sec. 2, 2. See also U.S. Minister Charles Eberhardt to State Department, July 20, 1928, Foreign Relations of the United States III (Washington: Government Printing Office, 1943), 444.

III

A Diplomat in Khaki Observes Nicaraguan Democracy

Looking for a Soldier Diplomat: The Municipal Elections of 1927

THE SEARCH FOR AN ABLE DIPLOMAT with experience in both civil and military affairs for the post of election supervisor began in the summer of 1927. Although they anticipated that selecting an army or marine officer would bring criticism from the Nicaraguan Congress and other opponents of the project, both Coolidge and Stimson were convinced a person with the combined talents of a military strategist and an effective negotiator had to be found.[1]

Generally, among administration circles, they thought the choice had to come from the ranks of military leaders who had served in areas where the United States had governed a foreign community. Perhaps the most notable of these "enlightened imperialists" was General Leonard Wood. Coolidge and Stimson agreed that Wood, who was then governor of the Philippines, embodied the ideal of a competent administrator with the discipline and dexterity needed for the sensitive and important task in Nicaragua. At the very best, Wood could be relied upon to select the most qualified officer from the ranks of his subordinates. Coolidge's special emissary, therefore, turned to the general for advice in appointing a soldier/diplomat for the Nicaraguan assignment. Wood took little time in making a recommendation. He suggested a trusted aide who had served

---

[1] Stimson, Diary entry, May 7-9, 1927. See also Kamman, *Search for Stability,* 138, for a brief account of U.S. Marine Commander Logan Feland's and Admiral Julian Sellers' thoughts on appointing a North American army general as election supervisor.

under him for many years in various duties, especially managing United States overseas possessions since 1898. He advised Stimson that General Frank Ross McCoy, his protegé, who had fought in the Spanish-American War, the Philippines, and World War I, was an ideal candidate. McCoy was a prominent member of a group of officers and civilians who in the 1920s thought that the United States was destined to play an active role in global affairs after World War I. Men like Stimson, Wood, and McCoy thought the sooner North American contacts — economic as well as political — were widened, the more stable and secure the uncertain 1920s would become. Wood considered McCoy an able military officer who could be relied upon to deal effectively with a local civilian government. Actually, Stimson had long since considered McCoy "his real chief of staff and best informed military advisor."[2]

General McCoy had worked with Wood for a number of years in various assignments. Certainly being married to Wood's niece did not impede his promotion and selection in a series of challenging and interesting posts. McCoy was a competent administrator, however, and a tactful diplomat who possessed unusual ability for assessing complicated situations, particularly in cases where U.S. military governments had to deal with civilian groups.

Soon after the Spanish-American War, McCoy joined Wood's staff in Cuba and assisted in laying the groundwork for a military government there. He succeeded in bringing some order and efficiency to the country in a relatively short time. The supervision of budgetary matters under General Wood provided him with valuable experience in an area which was to dominate relations between the United States and its Latin American neighbors from 1899 on.

When General Wood became governor of the Philippines in 1903, McCoy continued to serve his mentor in numerous posts there. He was briefly entrusted with the overall supervision and administration of the Moro Province and served on the legislative council there from 1904 to 1906. In 1911, as a member of the army general staff, McCoy participated in a

---

[2] Stimson to McCoy, October 20, 1927, McCoy Papers, Manuscript Division, Library of Congress, Washington, D.C.; A.J. Bacevich, *Diplomat in Khaki: Major General Frank Ross McCoy and American Foreign Policy, 1898-1949* (Lawrence: University Press of Kansas, 1989).

study of a proposed second canal through Central America.

Stimson was particularly anxious to have an election supervisor nominated as quickly as possible. He thought any delay in the matter would indicate indecisiveness in the foreign policy of the Coolidge administration, a stigma it had already acquired and could not afford in a North American presidential election year. Nor did he want anything to happen which would suggest to the Nicaraguan Liberals that the United States was reneging on its promise to restrict the powers of the Conservative government. Coolidge accepted Stimson's arguments for quick action and appointed McCoy less than one month after Díaz's "request" for election supervision.

On May 15, the Nicaraguan president formally asked the United States to supervise the 1928 election, according to the agreement between Stimson and Moncada. No one, not even Stimson, had as yet drawn up procedures for administering the project. As expected, the Liberals were apprehensive over prospects of limiting the vast powers of an incumbent party, and the Conservatives were concerned about potentially losing control of governmental machinery.[3] The United States' plans for policy implementation were simple. McCoy was directed to seek not the State Department's but Stimson's advice and counsel in the early stages of his mission. The Nicaraguan problem was to be in the hands of this unofficial adviser to the administration, and rather than Secretary of State Kellogg, McCoy was to make some of the key decisions regarding Nicaraguan matters in the months ahead.[4]

Stimson urged McCoy to visit Nicaragua, familiarize himself with the country's political situation, and make contacts with leaders of both parties. To obtain maximum cooperation for the United States, he advised McCoy to rely principally on the Liberal leaders for advice as they had conveyed an unqualified willingness to work for a United States-run election. In retrospect, this suggestion does not appear to have been a particularly wise one. The exclusion of Conservative leaders, especially Chamorro, from the initial discussions on how the election would be supervised created a solid and determined opposition to the passage of an

---

[3] Bernardo Sotomayor, *Informes sobre las Elecciónes de Autoridad Superiores* (Managua: Imprenta Nacional, 1928), 23.

[4] Stimson to McCoy, July 22,1927, McCoy papers, Manuscript Division, Library of Congress, Washington, D.C.

electoral law later on.[5]

In keeping with his legal approach to difficult political problems, Stimson urged the election board chairman to cultivate the friendship of Liberal party lawyers who might offer constructive suggestions for drawing up an electoral law in Congress—a critically important process for giving legal sanction to this new form of intervention avoiding direct U.S. military rule. The Stimson/McCoy correspondence clearly reveals the former's bias for the out party. He made no effort to instill a sense of objectivity in McCoy's task. Yet, Stimson's protegé had earlier experience directing the interests of the United States abroad. His career did not show that he had ever become unnecessarily and adversely involved with feuds and interparty rivalries in Cuba and the Philippines. He was to continue this practice in his Nicaraguan assignment but only after he had firmly established control over all political elements and administrative machinery in the republic.[6]

Stimson first suggested that McCoy observe the 1927 Nicaraguan municipal elections and determine how the government actually managed the electoral machinery. The U.S. Marines were to play only a secondary role in these early election contests, but were directed to make their presence conspicuous around voting booths in regions where either Liberals or Conservatives had the fewest registered voters. This display of "Yankee force" was designed to impress upon the Conservative majority the firm intention of the U.S. government to achieve a fair election later in 1928.

McCoy journeyed to Nicaragua in late summer 1927 and became familiar with many of the shortcomings and problems in these local elections. He also established contacts with Liberals as Stimson had suggested.[7] After the 1927 municipal elections, the Liberals showed concern over the undue control and partisanship from various chiefs of police in departments leaning toward the Conservative candidates. The *jefe político* (chief executive) of each department in the republic filled these law enforcement positions. Invariably, if a *jefe político* had been named by a Conservative president, the police chief in the local area would also be a member of the same party.

---

[5] Ibid., McCoy papers, June 1927.

[6] Ibid.

[7] Stimson and Bundy, *On Active Service*, 115.

Therefore, the Liberals urged that as a preliminary step to prevent fraud in the 1928 presidential election these policemen be removed. McCoy thought this request reasonable, so he suggested it might be worthwhile to establish U.S. police power in all the departments with the appointment of a North American officer from the planned marine-operated constabulary. Since marines would lead this indigenous military unit, it might serve as a major instrument in controlling the entire supervisory process.[8]

To effect this method of police control, the Nicaraguan Congress would have to approve a law that created a constabulary. Its passage was accurately predicted as a formidable task. In drawing up the National Guard agreement, details would be defined more clearly by the U.S. legation after McCoy had finished his inspection trip. However dim the prospects for the Congress passing a constabulary agreement, it is clear McCoy had every intention of removing police powers from the Conservative party from the beginning.

While the North American general chose to remain aloof from any participation in the municipal elections, the United States chargé was unofficially playing a very busy role in securing a degree of fairness in these local contests. The Liberals pressed for some limitations on the use of police power. In response, the United States legation suggested to the president that some of the more extreme cases of harassment and inconvenience the Liberals were being subjected to be ended.[9] For example, the administration required people to carry government-issued road passes. These cards indicated the bearer had paid "passage taxes" to the local government. The failure to obtain these documents prevented a voter from traveling to the election booth. The legation requested and received a promise from the chief executive that the collection of this "local revenue tax" would stop.[10]

Following the municipal elections, a number of alleged and fraudulent activities emerged which McCoy and the United States legation hoped to correct. In analyzing the total vote cast

---

[8] Kellogg to U.S. legation, Managua, Records, Department of State, hereinafter cited as RG 59, DF 817.00/5109, NA.

[9] Dana Munro to State Department, October 18, 1927, RG 59, DF 817.00/5082, NA.

[10] Ibid.

in all areas, except in the north and northeast departments where Sandino forces were most active, McCoy concluded the Liberals were in the majority and would have won sweeping victories if fairness had prevailed on election day. The failure of the Liberals to win any municipal elections convinced McCoy the Conservatives' unrestricted use of police power had to be eliminated. If this could be done, either directly by the marines or by the National Guard (constabulary), then the Liberals would have a chance to succeed at the polls in the 1928 presidential election. Since the Conservative-controlled Congress canvassed each department, the United States minister was convinced the incumbent administration was tampering with ballot boxes, particularly in cases where the election was close.

The vote-count procedure was destined to be an important issue in a feud between the Chamorrista Conservatives and the United States as the election supervisors moved in to take control of Nicaragua's internal affairs in early 1928.[11]

The 1927 municipal elections took place in an atmosphere of relative peace, primarily because of the large contingent of U.S. Marines (numbering 5,000 by March 1928). Since the Conservatives usually claimed the electoral victories, many party leaders believed future election procedures could be removed from the watchful eyes of the United States. Emiliano Chamorro had reached Managua in autumn of 1928, shortly before the municipal elections, with what McCoy described as his "shipload of monkey wrenches, ready to disrupt an orderly electoral process."[12] The former president quickly named candidates to committees for planning the municipal campaigns. This was a prelude to his upcoming battle with the United States electoral mission and later on the Díaz faction of his own party.

McCoy made an effort to meet with leading Conservative figures after the 1928 elections. Consequently, the Chamorristas were highly suspicious, and rightfully so, that McCoy had cooperated too closely with the Liberals. They were particularly sensitive to rumors the State Department would probably forbid their leader's quest for his party's nomination and prevent him from taking office if elected, which was correct. Conservatives viewed McCoy's aloofness as a sign of future

---

[11] Ibid., November 9, 1927, RG 59, DF 817.00/5132, NA.

[12] McCoy papers, letter to daughter, January 28, 1928, folder 2.

rejection of their efforts to win the presidential election, so they began to organize forces against the United States election project. They were convinced the Coolidge government wanted the Liberals to win since McCoy did nothing to placate Chamorro's followers during his sojourn in 1927. Consequently, a powerful wing of the Conservative party laid the groundwork to hinder, even prevent election supervision altogether and to do so by constitutional means. Paradoxically, a U.S. project for implementing democracy in Nicaragua was working but not in its interests. Moreover, General McCoy was not the least bit concerned about the growing menace of Sandino's activities. On one occasion in early 1928, the future election board chairman described the Nicaraguan rebel as "merely a slippery little fellow prowling among the mountains."[13]

Two Caudillos Seek Recognition

When Stimson secured a settlement in the civil war, Chamorro, then minister to France, was advised by his followers to return home. He launched a presidential campaign in both Washington and Managua with his principal agents, Chandler P. Anderson, a former State Department official turned lobbyist in the United States, and Nicaraguan Minister Alejandro César, who took steps to have the State Department accept him as a contender for the Conservative party's nomination and to recognize him if elected.

For some time the Department of State had viewed Chamorro as a disruptive influence in Nicaraguan politics. When he seized power in 1926, this opinion was reinforced. The U.S. government realized then his disregard for fair procedures in a presidential contest, and it realized it had to contend with a clever, pragmatic political figure. Secretary of State Kellogg was fully aware that the attractive and popular Chamorro wielded great influence in his party. More worrisome too, he had a better political organization than President Díaz. Consequently, the United States urged Conservatives to deny the former president the 1928 presidential nomination. Rejection by his own party would spare the North American republic the unpleasant task of denying him recognition later

---

13 *Washington Star*, May 13, 1928, sec. 2, 3.

on.[14] Therefore, a successful campaign to initiate a protest within the Conservative party against Chamorro was launched with the United States' blessing. As expected, it was not difficult to persuade Díaz to urge Chamorro to stay out of the race with the explanation that the latter's extreme partisanship would not lend itself to compromise and cooperation between the two major parties in the upcoming elections.[15]

While the United States legation prepared for election supervision with the concurrence of President Díaz, Anderson was urging the State Department to allow his political adversary, Chamorro, a chance to prove his good faith by being allowed a presidential candidacy. The North American chargé in Managua strongly urged the Department to take advantage of Chamorro's brief stay in Washington during early autumn of 1927 and inform him he would not be permitted to run for president. McCoy was certain that unless the Conservative leader was dissuaded from running while in Washington, it would be almost impossible to prevent his politicking in Nicaragua when he returned. The chargé also was convinced Díaz feared Chamorro's skill and popularity and thought Díaz would succumb to the pressures of Chamorro's forcible personality when he reached Nicaragua.[16]

Even if Chamorro were eligible to be a candidate, the United States chargé in Managua thought he should be denied the opportunity to run. The North American legation was certain his election would intensify the hostility between the two political parties and make the creation of a stable democratic government impossible. North American diplomats in Managua foresaw a chaotic political situation unless Chamorro was dealt with promptly and effectively.[17]

Anderson accompanied Chamorro to the State Department in early October 1927 to plead his case. They were advised quickly that the former president and Conservative leader would not be considered as a bona fide contender for his party's nomination nor would he be recognized if elected. This decision was based on strict legal grounds. U.S. officials

---

[14] Conservative members, Nicaraguan Congress to Chamorro, September 2, 1927, RG 59, DF 817.00/5054, NA.

[15] Ibid.

[16] Munro to State Department, October 4, 1927, RG 59, DF 817.00/5054, NA.

[17] Ibid.

argued that since Chamorro had been president during the term immediately preceding the 1928 election, he was disqualified as a candidate for election. Anderson pointed out the correct interpretation of this regulation was that the person must occupy the presidential office in the period directly preceding the election to be ineligible for office. Olds, the assistant secretary of state speaking for Secretary Kellogg, rejected this suggestion and all the pleas put forward by Chamorro and his U.S. adviser.[18]

As a result of Olds' confrontation with the former Nicaraguan president, the U.S. government also became suspicious of the activities of Alejandro César, Nicaraguan minister to the United States, who was busy seeking support for Chamorro. His partisanship posed some serious problems for the United States in the months ahead. After their appearance at the State Department to plead the former president's case, the activities of both men were watched closely as potential obstacles to this new aspect of U.S. policy in Nicaragua.

Having failed to obtain endorsement for the Conservative party nomination, an embittered Chamorro returned to Nicaragua. His partisans accorded him an exuberant reception which was noted with some trepidation by legation officials and President Díaz. Only a few knew the *caudillo* had been unable to obtain the State Department's blessing. The Conservative press noted the former president had come home only to work for his party and had no other political interests.[19] The Liberal newspapers, on the other hand, criticized the sincerity of his intentions and in numerous cartoons depicted him as a villain riding on the shoulders of a downtrodden people.[20]

The United States' exclusion of Chamorro from the presidential contest became widely known in Latin America and led to a considerable amount of criticism, adding to the sympathy already given Sandino in his anti-North American campaign. Many newspapers voiced indignation over the State Department's strong-arm approach. For example, a Buenos Aires paper commented:

---

[18] Anderson, Diary entry, October 9, 1927, Manuscript Division, Library of Congress (Washington D.C.).

[19] Managua *La Prensa*, November 27, 1927, 1. He was actually planning his next move in a strategy to limit the U.S. election supervision.

[20] León *La Noticia*, November 27, 1927, 1.

This episode demonstrates clearly that the elections to
which the Nicaraguan nation is called are going to be
'free,' in the sense that the authorities of Washington
use the word. They are going to be 'free,' but free of
obstacles for the designs that were put forward the day
on which the independent flag was taken down by the
invading country.[21]

The United States legation was relieved to learn that U.S.
officials had rejected Chamorro's candidacy and that had
precipitated discussions within the Conservative party on
selecting other candidates for the party's nomination. The
weapon of nonrecognition was still well understood by Central
American politicians. Some U.S. officials in Managua mistakenly thought Díaz would now have a strong voice in the future
selection of a Conservative candidate since Chamorro had
been put out of the picture. Yet Dana Munro, the United States
chargé, realized a presidential candidate supported by only
one faction in the Conservative party could not win an election.
He was convinced a settlement of differences by the Díaz and
Chamorro wings on a single candidate would enhance the
possibility of having equally divided forces in a two-party
race.[22]

As expected, Chamorro's partisans were outraged that he
had not been able to secure U.S. approval for his candidacy.
This resentment was exacerbated when they learned that
Moncada, the expected Liberal presidential candidate, had
journeyed to the United States in late 1927 and had been
greeted by Stimson at his New York home. The Chamorristas
then resolved to oppose actively the U.S. Nicaraguan election
supervision project. While on his New York pilgrimage,
Moncada had pressed Kellogg and Stimson to insist on
removing all police power from Díaz and promptly creating a
permanent, nonpolitical national guard.

Stimson was not at all concerned with the adverse
reaction arising from his attention to the Liberal leader during
his visit. He discounted State Department misgivings over this
outward display of support. He vehemently opposed taking

---

[21] Buenos Aires *La Prensa*, October 24, 1927, 1.

[22] Munro to State Department, December 26, 1927, RG 59, DF
817.00/5263, NA.

any steps, as suggested, to rebuff Moncada, conveying the United States' impartiality. Furthermore, for the Moncada detractors, Stimson recalled that the civilian-turned-general had supported the U.S. proposal for a supervised election at a time when it was not a particularly popular stand to take. Stimson thought Moncada should have been rewarded sooner in some fashion for his willingness to end the civil war. Consequently, Nicaraguan Conservatives and other observers, both in the United States and Latin America, correctly concluded that the reception given Moncada was tacit approval for his candidacy by the Coolidge administration.[23]

Eberhardt believed Moncada had made the trip to capitalize on his earlier contacts with Stimson and to convey the idea back home he had been chosen by the United States. The legation had actually requested that Moncada be dissuaded from making the journey, but Kellogg rejected the suggestion.[24]

Munro was particularly concerned that the undue attention and consideration given Moncada, a man whom he considered to be "low in moral character and integrity," would discourage efforts by many Nicaraguans to assist in the operation of an impartially run election. North American diplomats concluded that if one candidate had obtained U.S. support, then McCoy's efforts later on, as the national election board chairman, would not be taken seriously.

The principal result of Moncada's trip to the United States was the strengthening of Conservative opposition in the Nicaraguan Congress. Chamorro stood firm in opposing any measure dealing with United States supervision of the 1928 election. In fact, many Díaz supporters who had earlier agreed to the project turned to Chamorro as their only chance to prevent a Moncada victory with the perceived concurrence and support of the State Department. Clearly, Stimson's approval of Moncada's visit had been a U.S. tactical error. The Nicaraguan Congress would be a formidable rallying point for opponents to McCoy's assignment.[25] A number of issues would soon appear which Chamorro used to obstruct a major U.S. diplomatic objective — an impartially supervised election in autumn

---

[23] Stimson to Assistant Secretary of State Francis White, September 23, 1927, RG 59, DF 817.00/5043, NA.

[24] Eberhardt to State Department, September 8, 1927, RG 59, DF 817.00/5022, NA.

of 1928.

President Díaz, as expected, pledged unqualified support to the U.S. election project. But Chamorro, who found his political ambitions thwarted by the plan, naturally refused to cooperate with the incumbent Conservative administration. Consequently, he decided he would find his own candidate to run as the Conservative standard bearer. His choice, of course, would be someone responsive to his dictates. When learning of the Conservative *caudillo's* strategy, North American diplomats in Managua advised the State Department that a nominee from the Chamorrista group could never command enough support, either in the Conservative party or nationally. Well before the supervised elections were to begin, they concluded Chamorro's tactics would ultimately lead to a Liberal party victory in 1928 and effectively impede the passage and implementation of an electoral law granting the United States authority to run the presidential contest.[26]

---

[25] Stimson to Department of State, Official Papers, Yale University, October 4, 1927.

[26] Munro To State Department, December 26, 1927, RG 59, DF 817.00/5263, NA.

IV

The End Justifies the Means: Washington Confronts a Nicaraguan Congress

The Battle For 'Legalized Intervention'

PRESIDENT DÍAZ DID NOT EXPECT to participate in any deliberations which would draw up a revised electoral law. He thought the 1924 electoral law (Dodds Law) was still in effect as it provided for registration in all parts of the country by spring 1928. But the unsettled conditions in the north, which the Sandino movement had created, prevented chances for organizing a registration drive there. Equally important and significant, the United States planned to control the nation's entire electoral machinery in 1928, based on the guidelines set forth by the 1924 law.[1]

Yet President Díaz wanted the State Department to provide him with any new aspects of an electoral law if, in fact, one was to be drawn up. He was keenly aware of the pending congressional opposition to the supervision project and wanted to prepare his case to secure passage. Díaz's cooperation in an effort to push through a bill creating the National Guard in late 1927 had not endeared him to the Chamorrista wing of his party. The president took note that plans were being made in Congress to remove his negotiating power to deal with a foreign government in a constitutional issue.[2] Consequently, to

---

[1] Munro to State Department, RG 59, DF 817.00/5103, NA. The Sandino forces were operating outside of Matagalpa, and the Conservatives were suggesting that, in light of the unsettled conditions, the Nicaraguan Congress should reject the proposed election law. See also Kamman, *Search for Stability*, 156.

[2] Managua *La Gaceta Oficial*, January 1928, 7.

prepare the way for an early "political offensive," the president awaited some word from the State Department regarding major provisions, if any, to the already existing law.

Dr. Harold Dodds, a political science professor, secretary of the National Municipal League, and author of the 1924 election law, worked closely with General McCoy and the State Department during October and November 1927, drafting changes for administering Nicaragua's 1928 political contests. Essentially, the 1928 law granted extensive powers to the chairman of the Nicaraguan election board. It had not done so in the 1924 supervised elections. This was particularly discernible in procedural matters and the arbitration of disputes between party members on local boards during registration and the election itself.[3]

The law drawn up in the United States granted McCoy considerable power. For instance, he was invested with the right to overrule any decision made by either the Conservative or the Liberal party representatives on the national board. This prerogative was also given to every departmental and cantonal (precinct) board chairman, all of whom, were to be U.S. citizens. To insure the Nicaraguan members of the national and departmental boards were cooperative and amenable to the national chairman's wishes, the State Department suggested McCoy also be given the right to appoint all election board representatives. This would encompass the national board as well as the local ones. In other words, McCoy would be granted vast appointive powers, far more than the 1924 law. In the proposed 1928 project, the national election board, unlike the 1924 document, would allow McCoy to run the election.

This provision was expected to be one of the major items which would arouse Chamorrista opposition. Even Dodds saw the danger in granting the North American chairman this unlimited power to appoint all board members. He instead recommended the executive committees of the major political parties appoint representatives to the national and local boards. The State Department accepted Dodds' misgivings as well founded and consequently withdrew its proposal to grant McCoy these unlimited appointive prerogatives. However, the national election board chairman would still retain the right to call a meeting of the board even if the two other members from

---

[3] Assistant Secretary of State Francis White to Harold W. Dodds, October 29, 1927, RG 59, DF 817.00/5103, NA. Disputes challenging the voter's right to vote were expected.

the Liberal and Conservative parties did not attend. Therefore, he could decide issues by himself without interference. The basis for this extraordinary and unprecedented authority theoretically was justified on the ground that the need for prompt action could be delayed by the absence of one or both party members.

The electoral law had structural arrangements similar to the 1924 Dodds regulation, except all 13 departmental board chairman would be appointed by the national chairman. As in the 1924 law, three members would comprise the national board, the U.S. chairman and one representative each from the Conservative and Liberal parties. The 13 departmental boards would have a similar arrangement, under the close supervision of the national board chairman. The cantonal boards would also have three members, and their activities would come under the management of the departmental boards. The cantons, or *mesas* (precinct tables), would each be assigned the registration and voting supervision of some 500 people.

In deciding to allow the Conservative and Liberal parties to select both representatives on all election boards, the United States conceded to the architect of the 1924 law. This was done again at Dr. Dodds' urging, to avoid objections which were expected to arise if the original provisions were promulgated. Actually, the present membership and the chairmanships of the departmental and cantonal boards were based on the success of one of the parties in the preceding 1927 election. Liberal party leaders insisted they retain chairmanships of many departmental boards in areas where they had won election majorities. The United States rejected this suggestion; they feared Conservatives would demand the same privilege, holding a majority on the election boards and leaving McCoy with no supervisory control. In sum, he decided neither a Liberal nor a Conservative party member would be allowed to head any election board.[4]

The United States also insisted it retain the right to canvass all votes after the election. This provision was destined to provoke considerable discontent in the Nicaraguan Congress. The constitution of the republic specifically granted this right to the legislative branch.[5] As a result, Chamorro was handed a

---

[4] State Department to Munro, November 19, 1927, RG 59, DF 817.00/5152, NA.

[5] *La Constitucíon de Nicaragua*, March 4, 1912, art. 87, Archivo Nacional (Managua).

good issue to buttress his arguments for drastically limiting a supervised election. He would exploit it effectively by organizing a campaign to oppose the passage of the 1928 electoral law. The Chamorrista faction in Díaz's party looked forward confidently to a congressional battle, for they knew that in a joint session of the two houses, the Liberals were short of a majority by some 12 to 15 votes. Chamorro planned to organize his supporters and present the United States with a series of major legal obstacles in its attempts to wrest this canvassing prerogative from the legislative branch. The North American government then decided to launch its own campaign for the passage of the bill by working closely with President Díaz, who unqualifiedly supported a canvassing provision in the proposed electoral law.

Carlos Cuadra Pasos informed the State Department he wanted the United States to take full control of the election and grant McCoy the right to canvass votes. Actually, Cuadra Pasos was not enthusiastic about every aspect of the U.S.-proposed electoral procedures. He recognized the need for some independent and nonpartisan element to prevent one of the parties from administering the nation's election machinery, but he also realized if Chamorro gained control of the Conservative party his own chance for winning the presidential nomination might be irretrievably lost. Therefore, the foreign minister chose to accept the supervised election completely with the hope of being selected as the State Department's candidate.

Cuadra Pasos was well versed in hemispheric politics, particularly in diplomatic relations with the U.S. government. He was considered by many as Nicaragua's chief "internationalist." In any case, he became the United States' main strategist in the campaign to maneuver an election law through the Nicaraguan Congress. It appears Cuadra Pasos thought prospects for U.S. support of his unannounced presidential bid had improved. He suggested at one point an "election board dictatorship" be created, replacing President Díaz with a United States-appointed high commissioner to govern Nicaragua, "relieving the Conservative party of all responsibility and placing them on an equal footing with the Liberals in the political campaign."[6]

As expected, political considerations were behind Cuadra Pasos' suggestion to have the Conservative party completely

---

[6] Carlos Cuadra Pasos, "Intervencion," *Revista Conservadora del Pensamiento Centroamericano* (May 1962): 18.

abdicate all responsibility in election supervision. Specifically, it would absolve them from expected charges of "giving away Nicaragua's sovereignty" with the approval and adoption of the election law. His second objective was to dislodge Chamorro from party control.[7] The State Department rejected Cuadra Pasos' suggestion for a high commissioner and proposed instead a Nicaraguan as interim chairman of the national election board, who would step aside for General McCoy when the president of Nicaragua made his final appointment later on.[8]

Chamorro was fully aware of the close ties Carlos Cuadra Pasos and Díaz were developing with the U.S. legation. The Conservative leader then set about to make his first move by urging that the United States' right to canvass the election vote be excluded from the proposed election law. His tactics were to prove masterful. He proposed the creation of a constituent assembly, which presumably would make the necessary changes in the constitution to allow the national election board the right to canvass votes. Chamorro was certain he could win a majority of seats in a new assembly. Both the foreign minister and the president knew it, too. In fact, Cuadra Pasos informed North American envoy Eberhardt that this was a perfectly legal course to take, particularly if any part of the republic's constitution had to be changed.[9]

The dangers in convoking a constitutional convention were evident to the North American legation. The United States chargé feared a body of this kind would inevitably fall into the hands of the Chamorrista faction. If this occurred, then provisions in the constitution that provided for an election in 1928 would be removed altogether. Still worse, the assembly might elect a new president and outmaneuver the U.S. government entirely.[10] To force a Conservative party split, Cuadra Pasos was successfully prevailed upon to dissuade his friends in Congress from taking this unusual step in accordance with Chamorro's wishes. Moreover, the U.S. legation on this occasion and others began to rely more on the foreign minister than

---

[7] Dispatch, Munro to State Department, Stimson, Official Papers, Yale University, October 13, 1927, Photocopy. This and several copies of dispatches were sent to Stimson, keeping him abreast of election procedures.

[8] Ibid.

[9] Ibid.

[10] Ibid.

the president in dealing with the Nicaraguan Congress. The president was considered too weak in the use of executive powers, a characteristic he had frequently displayed in the past. On more than one occasion he threatened to resign simply because his colleagues were putting too much pressure on him to be more independent of U.S. directives. He also was concerned that cooperation in securing the adoption of the 1928 electoral law was actually against the best interest of his own party by giving the Liberals a reasonably good chance to win through their participation on all electoral boards.

Cuadra Pasos then appeared to be the most effective, reliable figure to work for passage of the law. Undoubtedly, his political ambitions had something to do with his lobbying efforts in the Congress at the behest of the United States.[11] The United States now faced two insurgencies: Sandino's armed resistance and Chamorro's legal war in Congress.

North American diplomats in Managua asked the Department of State to issue a communique to "interested parties" — meaning key political leaders in Nicaragua — asking them to pledge continued support for President Díaz. It read, in part, "This government could not fail to view with the utmost disapprobation any such disturbance of the status quo in the retirement of Díaz."[12] The die was cast. Secretary of State Kellogg took the opportunity to reject firmly any rumor that the department might accept the convocation of a constituent assembly. He wanted this fact known, especially to influential congressmen.[13] Meanwhile, a group of distinguished Nicaraguan lawyers who had been asked to review the proposed election law reported to the U.S. legation that the creation of an assembly was clearly within the framework of the constitution. The lawyers went a step further and vigorously attacked the proposed 1928 election law, saying:

> If the government of the United States of America has had the kindness to accede to the request of the government of Nicaragua to lend friendly assistance and to supervise the elections of the Highest Authority which are to be carried out in 1928, it must be borne in mind that the same government of the

---

[11] Ibid.

[12] Ibid., December 2, 1927.

[13] Ibid.

United States has shown repeatedly in a very clear and decisive manner that it desires that Nicaragua persevere in the constitutional path, that it desires her to learn to persevere in that path: and that its whole interest is that the government...be elected without violating the constitution. Therefore, it is our opinion that the Transitory Electoral Law [of 1928] cannot be proclaimed while the constitution which governs us remains in force. Nearly all of it [the Transitory Electoral Law] in its entirety and in its parts, is contrary to our fundamental charter.[14]

The memorandum also objected to the provision which required the chairman of the national electoral board be a U.S. citizen, appointed by Nicaragua's chief executive. They urged that the traditional procedures be adhered to, namely that the nation's Supreme Court appoint the presiding official of the election board. They thought the proposed electoral law was a clear violation of Nicaragua's sovereignty and an unwarranted removal of a regular judicial prerogative. The lawyers also claimed a constituent assembly could be fully empowered to deal with this matter. Paradoxically, Stimson's plan for democracy was working but not in the interest of the United States.

Dana Munro, in charge of the United States legation during the temporary absence of Minister Charles Eberhardt, was directed to reject the lawyers' protests and give them no further consideration. The U.S. diplomatic mission proceeded to submit the new law directly to Congress, relying in part on the persuasive powers of the weak and indecisive Díaz but more on the politically astute Carlos Cuadra Pasos. Washington believed the risks of a constituent assembly were too great as its convocation might very well eliminate all chances to supervise an election and enable Chamorro to wield unlimited power in domestic affairs.[15]

In an effort to neutralize the Chamorrista Conservatives in Congress, Munro proceeded to strengthen the Liberal position in an unprecedented manner. He permitted the national

---

[14] Nicaraguan lawyers to U.S. legation, Managua, December 31, 1927, RG 59, DF 817.00/5272, NA.

[15] Munro to State Department, December 29, 1927, RG 59, DF 817.00/5270, NA.

election board to appoint Liberals as presidents of departmental boards in the areas where the party had achieved a majority in the municipal elections in autumn, 1927. It appears this step was taken without State Department approval. But the North American diplomat thought it placed the United States in a more advantageous position to protect the Liberals now that hopes of passing the electoral law in Congress had diminished. Munro also wanted the Liberals to be in a position to have some voice in the coming registration procedures if the United States could not administer the election boards alone.[16] Munro had another motive in his move to help the Liberals: he wanted to show the Chamorrista Conservatives that unless they cooperated in the passage of the law, the United States was prepared to give the Liberal party an early active role in preparing election procedures.[17]

An Electoral Law 'With No Teeth' Bypassed Congress

When prospects for passage of the law grew dimmer in early 1928, the United States legation decided to have the enormously popular hero Charles Lindbergh appear before the Nicaraguan Congress during his trip through Central America and appeal for election supervision. The tumultuous welcome the North American aviator had received in Managua was expected to have a persuasive effect on project opponents. In his address to a joint session of the Nicaraguan Congress, Lindbergh pleaded for the restoration of peace and order in the republic under what he called "the guidance of the United States." But Lindbergh's charm had no effect on many of the senators and deputies. The Chamorristas were not dislodged from their position by Lindbergh's appeal.[18]

The 1928 election law passed (16 to 8) the Nicaraguan Senate on March 7. This occurred only because the Liberals and

---

[16] Ibid. Dispatch, U.S. legation, Managua, to State Department, Yale University, Photocopy; Stimson, Official Papers, December 29, 1927.

[17] Ibid. Foreign Minister Carlos Cuadra Pasos attended the Havana Conference in February 1928 and prepared a new draft of the proposed election law of 1928. He did so there with the U.S. delegation by simply re-wording the Dodds/McCoy provisions. The foreign minister returned home on a North American warship and promptly submitted the new bill to the Senate. See Kamman, *Search for Stability*, 158.

Díaz Conservatives were in control of the upper chamber. However, the law's fate was quite different in the Chamber of Deputies where Chamorro's partisans were in control. Members of the United States legation lobbied Congress by counting votes and setting recess dates. This intense activity proved futile, as the Díazistas and Liberals were not able to gather enough votes to pass it as originally drawn up. The measure was defeated on March 13 by a vote of 24 to 18. An electoral law did emerge but only in truncated form and re-designed by Chamorro and his adherents. It allowed only the congress, not the president, to appoint all electoral boards. The architect of the revised draft in the lower house was satisfied that at least some improvement had been made in election proceedings, but in Chamorro's words, "It really had no teeth."[19] Congress then adjourned *sine die*. Chamorro had his revenge.

The amended version passed by the Chamber of Deputies stipulated that U.S. members of the departmental and cantonal boards would serve only in an advisory capacity, as they had done in 1924.[20] Furthermore, the Chamorro substitute law stated that the intervention of the various U.S. assistants would cease altogether during the presidential contest, and only Nicaraguans would conduct the election proceedings.[21] North American election supervisors, who had been vested with powers in the Díaz-sponsored law, were to be mere observers, and, as expected, Congress would retain its canvassing prerogative. The Chamorro Conservatives were anxious to retain this right, particularly if the United States planned to support the Liberals, as César frequently reported from Washington.[22]

The defeat of the election law left the State Department and legation diplomats frustrated and confused. The major portion of the blame for its failure was placed on the hapless Díaz, who claimed to be physically ill most of the time. The United States chargé d'affaires was convinced that the president had not made a real effort to put pressure on the deputies in the lower house for passage of an electoral law drawn up by

---

[18] Managua *La Gaceta Oficial*, February 19, 1928, 2.

[19] Emiliano Chamorro, interview with author, Managua, April 7, 1965.

[20] Managua *La Gaceta Oficial*, January 17, 1928.

[21] Ibid.

[22] Munro to State Department, January 13, 1928, RG 59, DF 817.00/5762, NA.

Washington.[23]

The State Department, in a drastic step, decided to draw up an executive decree embodying the basic provisions of the original 1928 law and proclaiming its authority to run the presidential election. The legal basis for the new proposal was the Tipitapa agreement to which Moncada and Stimson had agreed in May 1927 and which Cuadra Pasos had accepted in the name of the Díaz government. Did this reflect the concurrence of the Conservative party? As events have shown, it clearly did not. The new decree envisioned the adoption of supreme and absolute powers vested in Díaz, which Minister Eberhardt doubted he could handle. Because the legation and the State Department had little confidence in the president, they planned to have McCoy assume full, unrestricted powers for election supervision.[24]

The United States suspected Díaz might not go along with the plan to circumvent Congress and decided to take matters in its own hands and give General McCoy full powers to maintain order and hold the election. Moreover, it was determined that under no circumstances would César, Nicaragua's envoy in Washington and Chamorro's protagonist in the United States, be informed of the plan. On far too many occasions the United States had used regular diplomatic channels and worked through the minister only to learn later that he had distorted department policy and then used it to his and Chamorro's advantage in Nicaragua.[25]

President Díaz, who was familiar with U.S. persistence, reluctantly decided to accept the new plan. He agreed to relinquish his executive power and accept the abrogation of a congressional role in the election only if the State Department promised not to make its intentions known publicly. Above all, the president stressed he did not want his acquiescence revealed prior to the adjournment of Congress and especially until Chamorro backers could be ousted from the cabinet. This seemed to be a reasonable proposal, so the United States went along with it.[26]

---

[23] Ibid.

[24] Memorandum, Department of State, March 2, 1928, RG 59, DF 817.00/5444-1/2, NA.

[25] Ibid., The State Department thought César failed to make clear its interests in the approval of the election law. See Munro to State Department, January 16, 1928, Rg 59, DF 817.00/5276; see also State Department to Munro, January 17, 1928, RG 59, DF 817.00/5276, NA.

After Díaz had been persuaded of the need for issuing an executive decree, the Department of State sent a dispatch to Eberhardt and McCoy containing the new law's provisions. The items in the bill were to be kept secret. If Congress persisted in rejecting the election law, then McCoy was instructed to release it.[27] The message stated all compromise proposals previously suggested which had reduced U.S. electoral supervisory powers were to be discarded. Under no circumstances did the United States want this new law's implementation conditional on the Nicaraguan Congress's approval.[28] One of the main reasons behind the decision to issue it was Sandino's raids, which in the spring of 1928 spread across the country's northern section, particularly in the Department of Jinotega. Even though the marines were consolidating their control over most of the country, security needs were still important, especially for administering the elections. Larger strategic interests also were becoming important as Sandino gained support from the international community, a development that the United States observed warily.

A firm hand was needed for the government to maintain political stability and insure U.S. cooperation in light of rebel activity. Moreover, the Coolidge administration wanted to lay the groundwork for a free election without obstruction from either the Nicaraguan Congress or the United States Congress, where criticism mounted over the entire intervention project. Consequently, if Díaz were vested with dictatorial powers, the United States could undertake a more vigorous campaign against the Sandino forces without political collapse in Managua resulting from congressional-executive wrangling there and in the United States.[29]

The decision to issue the executive decree on March 2, 1928, caused much anxiety in the legation as to the strategy the Chamorristas would adopt. To strengthen Díaz's position

---

[26] Eberhardt to State Department, March 15, 1928, RG 59, DF 871.00/5466, NA.

[27] Ibid., March 18, 1928, RG 59, DF 817.00/5475 (articles of decree were listed here), NA.

[28] Olds to McCoy and Eberhardt, March 14, 1928, RG 59, DF 817.00/5466, NA.

[29] Eberhardt to State Department, March 27, 1928, Department of State, records of the United States electoral mission to Nicaragua, 1928-1932, RG 43, folder D-5-C, NA. See also *Foreign Relations of the United States*, 1928, vol 3, 462-463.

against the Chamorro faction and to insure better cooperation from the Nicaraguan government, McCoy and Eberhardt decided to insist on the creation of a more cooperative cabinet. Two members of the Díaz faction in the Conservative party had worked closely with Chamorro to defeat the electoral law. Their positions, as heads of the ministries of public instruction (propaganda and education) and *fomento* (police and internal revenue collection), had increased the congressional opponents' advantage. If loyal Díaz followers could be placed in these important positions, the United States could then proceed with a program for election supervision.

Consequently, the legation made a list of prospective candidates for these posts and sent it to the Department of State for examination and selection.[30] Apparently, the legation had chosen the candidates carefully; Kellogg was satisfied that any of the persons proposed would be acceptable. As a result, Orontes Lacayo, a Díaz supporter, was made minister of *fomento* (development). His selection seems to have been predicated almost solely on his developing dislike for Chamorro.[31] Juan J. Díaz, a close friend and confidant of Carlos Cuadra Pasos, was made minister of public instruction. This post was extremely important to the United States, as he would oversee registration and voting procedures. However, after the defeat of the electoral law in Congress, they learned that Ruiz was an active Chamorro sympathizer and supporter.

A cabinet without troublemakers was created. A loyal group of Díaz followers now held posts in the administration. For the most part they would be amenable to an active U.S. role in the country's internal affairs in 1928. This was the only way Washington considered a free, impartially supervised election possible.[32]

---

[30] Ibid.

[31] Ibid.

[32] Virgilio Guandian, *Memoria de la Gobernación y Anexos 1927-1928* (Managua: Tipografía y Encuadernación, 1928), Archivo Nacional, 17.

V

Liberals and Conservatives: Pliable and Contentious

A Political Revolution

For some time since the fall of Liberal president José Santos Zelaya in 1909, the Conservative party happily had accepted North American support to remain in power. On the other hand, Liberals had experienced repeated frustration as an out party wishing to topple the entrenched opposition. Since political stability had been one of U.S. policy's principal goals in Nicaragua during the nineteenth and twentieth centuries, Liberal campaigns for public office had, for the most part, been sacrificed, especially since Zelaya's ouster in 1909, as one of their members described it in 1928, "on the high altar of peace and tranquility."[1] Yet by spring 1928, the Liberals realized that Stimson's commitment at Tipitapa had some meaning. Therefore, they urged the United States to provide elaborate safeguards for the free exercise of the franchise.

As expected, the Conservatives looked with misgiving on steps the Coolidge government had taken to control the republic through supervised elections and concluded that intervention now was to be more of a political nature, replacing a military occupation alone. They perceived this correctly as a major change in the nature of U.S. intervention. The Díaz regime was stripped of its numerous administrative and appointive powers during the summer of 1928. The incumbent administration realized the full meaning of this form of U.S. intervention, which would leave the structure of a government intact but control numerous administrative offices of the state.

At the 1927 Tipitapa conference, Stimson was sympathetic to Liberal leaders' complaints and deplored the only

---

[1] Managua *El Comercio*, April 18, 1928, 2.

means the out party had at its disposal to oust the entrenched Conservatives, namely by revolution or coup d'état.[2]

Coolidge's emissary personally believed the 1907 and 1923 Central American peace conferences had worked against the interests of the United States and particularly the Liberal party in Nicaragua. These meetings rejected revolution and coups d'état as vehicles for changing governments and assuming power. The 1907 and 1923 meetings prohibited military action in the quest for political control. This left Nicaraguan Liberals in a particularly difficult situation. Consequently, Stimson was convinced the Conservative party would not carry out the legal steps proscribed by Nicaraguan law. As long as the incumbent government retained control of the police force, collected revenues, and exercised other functions, it would remain in power indefinitely.[3]

As the United States assumed administrative power over the electoral machinery in early 1928, the Nicaraguan Liberal looked on skeptically. Liberal deputies and senators resigned themselves to succeed or fail at the polls on the merits of Stimson's promises to impose vigorously stringent laws for election supervision.[4] In an impassioned appeal to restrict Diaz's prerogatives, a Liberal leader expressed the attitude of his party — many of whom were anti-interventionists — when he told Stimson on one occasion, "I personally have an intimate conviction of your good intentions to do justice to the defenseless Liberal party of a small country which has, at times, been mistakenly judged with respect to its sentiments towards the United States."[5]

The North American legation and election officials embarked on a program to restrict the Conservative government's vast powers. Moreover, they established close relationships with Liberal party leaders. The major spokesman for the Liberal Moncada forces was Dr. Enoc Aguado, who played an active role as a mediator ending the civil war in spring of 1927. The U.S. diplomats considered the appointment of a Liberal as a secretary in the U.S. legation unwise, but to reassure Aguado

---

[2] Stimson, Diary entry, April 15, 1927.

[3] Ibid.

[4] Enoc Aguado to Henry Stimson, June 25, 1927, Record of U.S. Electoral Missions to Nicaragua, 1928-1932 (hereinafter cited as RG 43), Records, 1928 mission, folder M-3-10, NA.

[5] Ibid.

that the best interests of his party would be considered, they offered him a position on the national election board as Moncada's representative. He gratefully accepted and interpreted this gesture as a clear indication of U.S. determination to see that an impartially run election took place or, a more encouraging interpretation — that the U.S. government wanted the Liberals to succeed in the presidential contest.[6]

From the beginning, the U.S. government clearly was determined to assure the Liberals they had at least a good opportunity to capture the presidency. Furthermore, McCoy repeatedly promised a vigorous plan to deprive the autocratic Díaz government of its vast powers, particularly during an election, even if it meant disregarding the Nicaraguan Congress's power in approving an electoral law.

As far back as the Tipitapa agreement, the Liberals had presented the United States with a detailed plan to follow in order to check Conservative party activity during the 1928 election. The significant proposal provisions urged the United States to select the national election board chairman, prevent Congress from canvassing contest results, and lastly, insist that representatives of both parties be appointed to election boards in all 13 departments' precincts.[7] The United States accepted the suggestions in various forms and used them as the basic steps in its plan to restrict the powers of both the executive and legislative branches. For the first time, the Liberals were confident the Coolidge administration meant to keep the promises made in June 1927, when the executive decree included all their proposals.

Alternate representatives of the two major political groups were to be national election board members. A less noticeable *modus operandi* with the Liberal party leadership was undertaken. The North American advisory staff was directed to maintain contact with the party at its national convention held in February 1928. The initial meetings on this occasion were to serve as the basis for a continuing close relationship between the United States' electoral mission and the Liberal party from then on. While no staff members publicly endorsed the Liberals, a feeling of support for the party's cause became

---

6 Ibid.

7 "Suggestions regarding conduct of elections," Liberal party directorate to U.S. legation, Managua, n.d., RG 43, Records, 1928 mission, folder M-3-11, NA.

apparent. Moncada, then confident of success, prepared his program for the election campaign.[8]

The Liberal party convened on February 19-20 to nominate its standard bearer. General McCoy took the occasion to send Bruce Howe, a staff member, to view the proceedings and establish a party liaison. Prominent among Howe's first contacts was the *jefe político* in the department of León, Anastasio Somoza Garcia. Later he would become head of the National Guard, and Nicaraguan president Howe [1936-1956] described him as "a fine, genuine liberal." The *jefe político* was also a close confidant and loyal Moncada supporter. The Leon party leader assured Howe that General Moncada was the only serious contender for his party's nomination and that he would render unqualified cooperation to the United States in its election supervision when he was officially nominated.[9]

A very important project, later to be of inestimable value to the United States, was started at the Liberal convention. One of the fruits of the Somoza/Moncada/Howe meetings was a plan which arranged for Liberal party leaders to infiltrate the insurgent forces in areas where the rebel Sandino operated and thereby serve as excellent intelligence agents for the marines in the vicinity.[10] This strategy's second purpose was to organize Liberal partisans to counteract rumors of pending Sandino raids that the Conservatives were allegedly spreading, which placed many northern Liberal-dominated regions under a state of siege and caused elections to be cancelled.[11] On one occasion Chamorro suggested that disrupted areas (usually Liberal strongholds) be excluded from the election. This lent credence to rumors that his followers were playing a direct role in these insurgent activities. Howe, therefore, was particularly anxious for the infiltration project to be kept a secret as its revelation obviously would indicate too close an association with the Liberals. Failure to have made these same arrangements with the Conservatives indicated the United States suspected they were working with Sandino from time to time, a suspicion raised later on.[12] If the Conservatives had known of these U.S.

---

[8] McCoy to State Department, February 29, 1928, RG 43, folder P-4, NA.

[9] Memorandum, Walter Howe, staff assistant, U.S. electoral mission, February 18, 1928, RG 43, Records, 1928 mission, folder P-4, NA.

[10] Ibid.

ties with the Liberals in the early months of 1928, they may have rejected the supervised election program entirely.

Howe still found a considerable level of anxiety among the Liberals concerning U.S. sincerity in running a fair election. General Moncada was concerned about a press release in early February 1928, which quoted Carlos Cuadra Pasos as having suggested a coalition of both parties on one ticket as a solution to the Nicaraguan embroilment. Many Liberals who attended a meeting with Howe just before their convention believed this suggestion to be U.S.-backed and thought its revelation by Cuadra Pasos was used to test the reaction of Liberal leaders. Moncada did not believe Howe's denial of his country's complicity in the maneuver was strong enough. Howe had stated, in rather vague terms, that the United States would never express approval or disapproval of the selection of candidates for public office in Nicaragua.[13] Howe's rather ambiguous remark made the Liberal party leaders uneasy. They remembered Chamorro's failure to gain U.S. approval for his candidacy and wondered if this could be an attempt by the United States to revert to the Conservative/Liberal ticket of Solórzano/ Sacasa in 1924. The State Department was undoubtedly examining all kinds of solutions and wanted to see what the Liberal reaction would be. Whatever doubts lingered in the Liberals' minds, McCoy's emissary was able to establish a good relationship with Moncada and his followers like Somoza. Howe's later frequent visits with party candidates indicate, in many respects, the friendship that developed between the North American and the Liberal party leadership.[14]

Howe assured Moncada that General McCoy was prepared to go beyond mere election supervision, such as reporting election results, and establish complete control over the revenue collectorship and communications systems as well. After explaining the manner in which this would be done, Howe believed the Liberals were confident of U.S. support. The North American election board emissary also effectively discounted the coalition rumor, and the Liberal party chieftains apparently forgot or discounted it. At the opening of the Liberal party convention, the U.S. flag was displayed prominently in

11 Ibid.

12 Ibid.

13 Ibid.

14 Ibid.

the hall for Howe's benefit. Moncada was nominated with little opposition, and all party chieftains backed the candidate enthusiastically.[15]

Some three weeks before the convention, the U.S. legation learned from Liberal party sources that José Antonio Medrano, a political unknown, would be Moncada's running mate. They had notified North American authorities early to obtain their approval. Dana Munro, the chargé d'affaires, was not enthusiastic about this selection and considered Medrano a man of "little force and less character." However, he was pleased to learn the vice-presidential candidate was willing to cooperate closely with the United States.[16] Medrano was Moncada's first choice as a running mate. Others had been suggested to him, but most were unacceptable to the Liberal leader because of their well-known ambitions for the presidency. Consequently, Medrano was selected because he firmly expressed no higher political ambitions. His following was too small to threaten Moncada anyway.

Howe was present when General Moncada delivered his acceptance speech. He reported the activities in great detail. McCoy's emissary noted that the nominee immediately expressed his wholehearted support for a U.S. presence in Nicaragua. He began his address by stating that the Monroe Doctrine had to remain in effect "to preserve and protect Nicaragua's sovereignty." Moreover, the candidate noted that probable party success would depend solely on efforts by the North American government to restrict the Díaz regime in its drive to place a candidate in the presidency.[17] Moncada also expressed his opposition to a plan for creating a Liberal/Conservative ticket. He cited the failure of the 1923 coalition "to survive the maneuvers of overly ambitious politicians." This comment, of course, was directed at Chamorro and perhaps also to the politically ambitious Foreign Minister, Carlos Cuadra Pasos, who had first suggested the idea. The Liberal candidate praised the United States lavishly by suggesting Nicaragua's independence had been maintained through U.S. intervention. He concluded his acceptance speech by saying, "The doctrine

---

15 Ibid.

16 Munro to State Department, January 13, 1928, RG 59, DF 817.00/5611, NA.

17 Memorandum, Howe, February 19, 1928, RG 59, DF 817.00/5611, NA.

regarding our duty is to accept the influence of the United States of America, for progress, liberty, and civilization. The United States and Central America are slaves to reciprocal obligations."[18]

Unknown to McCoy and Howe, a meeting of the Liberal hierarchy took place in León during the convention. Leaders from all parts of the country warned Moncada that he could keep his party's nomination only as long as the United States was able to keep its promise and run the election. This incident may explain why the nominee voiced such praise for the Coolidge government. In retrospect, it is hard to believe these leaders thought Moncada could have been elected under any other circumstances than under the United States' watchful eye; a less cooperative candidate than Moncada might never have defeated his Conservative opponent.[19]

At the conclusion of the Liberal conclave, Howe was confident that good contacts had been made with the Liberals. Furthermore, he strongly recommended that a continuing association be maintained with them to "give their candidate a good chance to occupy the presidential chair."[20] Howe also revealed his belief in Moncada's likely success when he described the Liberal party as being "unified in one purpose and confident of victory if the United States adequately took control of Nicaragua's government."[21]

Howe's conferences with Liberal leaders at the convention surprisingly appear to have been kept secret. His dealings with the opposition marked a turning point in U.S. involvement in the country's domestic politics and especially during the election supervision period. Specifically, a change in the United States' policy of unqualifiedly supporting an incumbent regime took place. If McCoy had not intended to support Moncada, his assistance certainly provided everything short of outright endorsement. At the very least, the Liberals were confident of victory if the election board staff remained neutral and exercised its power and influence equitably.

---

[18] Managua *El Comercio,* February 21, 1928, RG 43, Records, 1928 mission, folder P-4, NA, Photocopy.

[19] McCoy to State Department, February 19, 1928, RG 59, DF 817.00/5438, NA.

[20] Memorandum, Howe, February 20, 1928, RG 43, Records, 1928 mission, folder P-4, NA.

[21] Ibid.

General Moncada was not content to allow the United States simply to observe his party's operations. He wanted the North American government to help draw up his economic and social program, which would be a guideline for his administration. He submitted the entire Liberal party platform with its agenda to the North American election board chairman for comment and approval; McCoy promptly examined and endorsed both.[22]

The two major parties' traditional policies were to change significantly in 1928. For years, the Liberals had strongly objected to any form of U.S. interference in the republic's internal affairs. Now the Coolidge/Stimson project was to offer Moncada a chance to cast out the entrenched Conservatives for an active role in Nicaraguan presidential politics but without replacing a civilian government. Of greater importance, the North American government was no longer looked upon as the harbinger of defeat to Nicaraguan Liberals. In fact, United States personnel in 1928 had pointedly conveyed the impression that if the Liberals succeeded at the polls, a fairly supervised election could be said to have taken place.[23]

Personalismo in the Conservative Party

The Liberal party welcomed McCoy's appointment as election board chairman. The Conservatives, on the other hand, saw their election chances immeasurably reduced as the North American-run electoral boards began to function, disregarding the once-proposed Chamorro law limiting a U.S.-supervised election.[24] The effort to pass a restricted election law resulted in a severe and damaging blow to the Conservative party's unity. At the outset of the civil war, the United States had decided to give wholehearted support to Díaz and to prevent a Liberal military campaign from ousting him. Later on, Díaz discovered he had to pay a price for this support. The success or failure in the creation of a new electoral law was placed almost entirely on his shoulders. He was, therefore, the vehicle through which the United States had maneuvered itself into the country's domestic politics while retaining a government structure.

---

[22] Moncada to McCoy, March 7, 1928, RG 43, Records, 1928 mission, Folder P-4, NA.

[23] Munro to Assistant Secretary Francis White, Department of State, April 18, 1928, McCoy Papers, Photocopy.

[24] Ibid.

Díaz's chief opposition came from the ranks of his own party as he tried to arrange for passage of the Tipitapa agreement. Chamorro was determined to create a case in defense of the Nicaraguan constitution which prohibited the Chamber of Deputies from delegating any of its authority to run an election. Although this tactic succeeded, it did great harm to the party. Its membership was divided into two camps: one supporting Díaz and his policy that accepted U.S. supervision with a limited executive role, the other rallying to the more popular and charismatic Chamorro who set out to destroy, or at least impede, the establishment of a new electoral law.

Díaz, who was already labeled as a North American "puppet," was watched carefully as he planned to control the Conservative party machinery. As expected, Carlos Cuadra Pasos, his personal choice for the presidential nomination, created considerable interest. Many thought his selection might be the United States' candidate too. Certainly, the Conservative press thought this way as this was the way Nicaraguan presidents had been nominated often in the past.[25]

Since the final electoral provisions did not pass the Chamorro-dominated Chamber of Deputies, the State Department had to decide if it was important to concentrate its effort bolstering the weak and indecisive Nicaraguan president and back him in his internal party battles. The latter possibility was clearly a dangerous tactic, and the North American legation was fully aware of it. The move was fraught with danger as it would draw a sharp division over party control among Conservatives. But the legation was prepared to risk this step rather than see the party fall under the absolute control of Emiliano Chamorro — a bitter critic of the United States' Nicaraguan policy.[26]

A heated debate erupted in the State Department over the question of how far the Coolidge government should go in its support of Díaz. The electoral law had failed to pass Congress, and some officials saw no need for helping him in an inter-party feud. Some U.S. diplomats wondered if it really made much difference who led the Conservatives as long as Chamorro was kept out of office.[27] Secretary of State Kellogg saw no need to express public support for Díaz. He thought it was the

---

[25] Ibid.

[26] Eberhardt to Kellogg, March 31, 1928, RG 43, Records, 1928 mission, folder D-5-C, NA.

president's duty to fulfill the obligations made at Tipitapa. Since the Conservative congress had rejected them, why, asked Kellogg, should the chief executive be praised and rewarded for failing to achieve an objective he was morally obligated to accomplish?

U.S. diplomats in Managua, on the other hand, urged unqualified support for Díaz. Eberhardt thought the president had risked leading his party to defeat when he publicly endorsed the electoral law. The legation believed, on that basis alone, he should be rewarded for his battle against Chamorro for party control. Moreover, Eberhardt and Munro were convinced that failure to back Díaz would indicate the United States was unsure of its position now that the electoral law had failed to pass Congress.[28] But Secretary of State Kellogg was to have his way. Rewards were not to be rendered unless deserved. The State Department decided to remain aloof from the Conservative feud, at least for the time being, and directed the legation to remain neutral.

Washington's failure to support President Díaz openly led Chamorro to believe that the North American government was unsure of its prospects for successful election supervision.[29] As a result, the former president began a campaign to re-impose his control over the party's rank and file. He set out to select his own candidate — one not dominated by either Díaz or the United States. Minister Eberhardt saw the inherent dangers in Chamorro's plans to select his own candidate, breaking with Díaz. The yankee diplomat was convinced that his government did not understand the hazards of this development. Both Eberhardt and Munro explained that if each faction in the Conservative party selected a candidate, no contender for the presidency could possibly gather a majority of votes required for election, in which case the constitution clearly provided that the Chamber of Deputies (in Chamorro's control), meeting in joint session with the Senate, would select a president. Eberhardt made a survey of the prospects for a Chamorro-dominated Congress in spring of 1928 and found, to his chagrin, that the former president would indeed have a

---

27 Kellogg to Eberhardt, April 2, 1928, RG 59, DF 817.00/5528, NA.

28 Eberhardt to Kellogg, March 31, 1928, RG 43, Records, 1928 mission, folder D-5-C, NA.

29 Chamorro proceeded to plan his strategy accordingly; interview with author, Managua, April 7, 1965.

substantial majority in the Nicaraguan legislature. The U.S. minister understood the motives behind Chamorro's effort to prevent the party from nominating one candidate.[30] This was the most important reason why North American diplomats in Managua finally decided to give official support to Díaz in his drive to dominate his party's councils. The legation saw how Chamorro's political tactics clearly would damage a Liberal campaign. Should a Conservative Congress ultimately select Nicaragua's chief executive, Moncada's chance for victory would be destroyed.[31]

Moncada tried for some time to bring this matter to U.S. attention. He pointed out that the traditional two-party system was in great danger in 1928. Moreover, unknown to many, a debate had developed in the Liberal party as to the advisability of discussing this problem openly. Some feared it might have reinforced the Chamorrista efforts to accomplish their objective.[32] Government newspapers under Díaz's direction and influence urged the Liberals to stay out of Conservative wrangling. The president feared if Moncada expressed too much concern it would encourage Chamorro to persist in widening the party split.[33]

In early April 1928, Chamorro made his first move to select his own presidential ticket. He proposed Vicente Rappaccioli, a wealthy landowner, but Eberhardt was not impressed with Chamorro's choice. He described the nominee as having "very little experience and intelligence whose only claim to political preferment appears to be his personal devotion to General Chamorro and his ability to make a large contribution toward the expense of the campaign."[34] The United States legation, therefore, had some misgivings about the Rappaccioli selection. It looked as if he had absolutely no chance to defeat Moncada. His selection merely meant a split in the Conservative party and a possible disruption of a United States-run election.

---

[30] Eberhardt to State Department, March 28, 1928, RG 59, DF 817.00/5808, NA.

[31] Managua *La Noticia*, May 26, 1928, 1.

[32] Managua *El Comercio*, May 27, 1928, 2.

[33] Managua *La Prensa*, May 27, 1928, 2.

[34] Eberhardt to State Department, March 24, 1928, RG 59, DF 817.00/5553, NA.

To pacify the Díazistas, Chamorro suggested the highly respected Foreign Minister Carlos Cuadra Pasos as the vice-presidential candidate. However, Díaz rejected the proposal. He refused to accept a secondary role in the party's councils with his cabinet officer running alongside a hand-picked Chamorrista. At this point in the pre-election maneuvering, Eberhardt and McCoy were convinced former president Chamorro firmly controlled the various Conservative executive committees in departments throughout the republic. They correctly ascertained that these party organizations were not prepared to back Díaz, who had earlier accepted a plan to restrict their vast powers in the 1928 election.[35]

Chamorro was convinced the United States had failed to maintain a neutral position in his feud with Díaz. Specifically, he suspected that Eberhardt had informed leaders in government circles that Cuadra Pasos was his choice for the Conservative presidential nomination.[36] Eberhardt believed Chamorro's prospects for success as the party's dominant figure seemed assured since a split appeared likely. Put simply, if the Conservatives could not select one candidate, then they would lose the general election to Chamorro, allowing him to assume leadership when the Díaz organization collapsed.

By May 1928, Chamorro had made good use of his long association with the party's rank and file members since Zelaya's fall in 1909. In all but two of the 13 departments, the former president had been able to elect delegates pledged to support Rappaccioli's candidacy. Moreover, the Chamorristas had appointed an alternate representative to the Conservative members on the national election board. This was done to show Díaz that his influence in that body was ending.[37]

As could be expected, the Nicaraguan president feared he would lose control of the party's national directorate and fail to have Cuadra Pasos nominated as his own presidential candidate. In a surprise move, Díaz ordered the Conservative

---

35 Ibid., April 10, 1928, RG 59, DF 817.00/5608, NA.

36 Emiliano Chamorro, "Autobiografia." Managua *Revista Conservadora de Pensamiento Centroamericano* (August 1960): 6. Chamorro says Díaz told him that Eberhardt wanted Carlos Cuadra Pasos. Julio Cardenal, the Conservative party vice-presidential nominee substantiated this story in Managua, interview with the author, March 5, 1965.

37 Eberhardt to State Department, April 10, 1928, RG 59, DF 817.00/5608, NA.

party national directorate committee to cease holding meetings. As chairman, he ordered it to stop examining the
credentials of rival delegations to the national convention.
McCoy's staff feared this high-handed act might well result in
armed clashes if the party directorate were denied its right to
settle differences between factions.[38] To its dismay, McCoy's
staff learned that Chamorro also controlled 11 of the 19
members on this governing body. The assistant U.S. national
election board chairman strongly urged intervening to prevent
Chamorro from solidifying his position. It seemed two Conservative conventions would be held, and this meant disaster for
a Liberal/Conservative contest in the general election.[39]

Eberhardt believed Díaz wanted the national election
board to intervene directly on his behalf, a step which a McCoy
staff member had already suggested. The president and his
followers could not conceive of a U.S. decision favoring
Chamorro because of his past opposition to election supervision. They concluded McCoy had no choice but to back
Foreign Minister Carlos Cuadra Pasos and support the president or pursue a far more difficult and potentially embarrassing
course and find a compromise candidate. The U.S. legation and
the election board's secretariat were also aware of this dilemma. One Chamorro-led Conservative faction was an avowed
opponent of election supervision altogether; the other, led by
Díaz, now was playing a role in public as being favored by the
United States. To make matters worse, it was feared if the State
Department supported Díaz in the Conservative wrangle,
Liberals would claim that the traditional policy of backing the
incumbent president was to continue.

Secretary of State Kellogg at first did not want to take a
position in the Conservative party conflict. He directed McCoy
not to interfere while the party still had a chance to resolve its
own internal problems. The secretary offered no recommendations as to how the party could unite behind one ticket. He
thought further opposition to U.S. presence in Nicaragua
would result if the national election board took on the burden
of resolving factional disputes. Yet, when the Chamorro/Díaz
conflict intensified in late spring, he authorized the election
board to intervene whenever attention had died down over

---

[38] Col. Francis Parker, vice chairman, Nicaraguan national election
board, to McCoy, May 17, 1928, RG 59, DF 817.00/5661, NA.

[39] Ibid.

Díaz's efforts to disregard the proper functions of his party's national directorate.[40]

President Díaz was not discouraged by Kellogg's initial decision to stay out of the feud. He proceeded to publicize his support for Cuadra Pasos, leaving McCoy and the legation still reasonably confident that the foreign minister had a better chance at the polls than Rappaccioli.[41] Obviously aware of the legation's position, Cuadra Pasos asked the North Americans to disavow publicly the Chamorro faction. This plea for direct intervention failed, primarily because the legation believed it would permanently impair any future chances for mending party wounds.[42] Yet the numerous conferences between Díaz and the legation regarding the former's request to back Cuadra Pasos did not go unnoticed. The Liberal press denounced what it incorrectly concluded to be United States' support for Díaz's candidate.[43]

Eberhardt agreed with the Liberals' view; namely, if the president were allowed to pick his own candidate, thereby disregarding the party's deliberations, a Conservative/Liberal contest was not likely to take place. The U.S. minister suggested Díaz be warned that Washington could withdraw diplomatic recognition if he followed this tactic and personally nominated his foreign minister, Carlos Cuadra Pasos. The legation decided to send the president their threat in a communique, mentioning that his actions were "an unnecessary step at a time when his authority depends so completely upon the support he was receiving from the United States."[44]

Unable to obtain the United States' unofficial endorsement for Cuadra Pasos, Díaz embarked on a vigorous campaign to have the Conservative party nominate a candidate of his choice. The United States did not look on the chief executive's active, energized political role favorably. McCoy thought that the Cuadra Pasos candidacy was an attempt on the president and foreign minister's part to show the latter's

---

[40] Kellogg to Legation, Managua, March 24, 1928, RG 59, DF 817.00/5553, NA.

[41] Ibid.

[42] Ibid.

[43] Managua *El Comercio*, April 14-15, 1928, 1; and Managua *La Noticia*, April 14, 1928, 2.

[44] Eberhardt to State Department, April 16, 1928, RG 59, DF 817.00/5610, NA.

candidacy was an outgrowth of his U.S. contacts. Consequently, the legation changed its course and searched for a
compromise candidate within the Conservative party.[45]

While disregarding Minister Eberhardt's warnings not to
endorse a candidate, Díaz was confident that the United States
could not support Chamorro anyway. So in a rare display of
independence, the president held his own convention in
Managua on May 20, 1928, to nominate Cuadra Pasos. The U.S.
election mission sent one of its members to observe the
proceedings as McCoy wanted a careful report of the events.
The United States observer's activities at this conclave were far
different from those conducted at the Liberal gathering a few
months earlier. McCoy's emissary to the Díaz convention was
instructed to observe the deliberations only and not make
personal contact with any of its leaders.

The Díaz assembly met simply to confirm the candidacy
of Cuadra Pasos. Nothing indicated that the president had
made the slightest attempt to create even a facade of a
democratic proceeding.[46] The foreign minister was nominated
by "unanimous applause," as a McCoy staff member caustically
described it. Cuadra Pasos proclaimed in his acceptance
speech that as a "God-fearing man, the eyes of the Almighty"
were always upon him, watching his every move. He went on
to say, "...in this critical period of the country's history, when
the party has called upon the United States to supervise the
election, I will be the instrument of God's will by bringing
peace to Nicaragua and seek the nation's highest office
hopefully through the blessings of God's hand."[47]

Díaz made full use of his office to solidify support for
Cuadra Pasos as he embarked on a purge campaign, removing
Chamorro sympathizers from public office. Moreover, the pro-
government paper, *La Prensa*, in an attack on the Chamorro
faction, pointedly observed an electoral law provision stipulat-
ing that unless a Conservative candidate had notified the
government of his intention to seek the presidential nomination by April 15, 1928, his name could not appear on the
general election ballot. This obviously disqualified Rappaccioli
as he had not been a registered candidate until late April.[48]

---

45 Ibid., March 24, 1928, RG 59, DF 817.00/5553, NA.

46 Memorandum, Cuadra Convention (Managua), May 20, 1928,
RG 43, Records, 1928 mission, folder P-2-A, NA.

47 Ibid.

At the time the Díaz convention met in Managua, Chamorro delegates convened in Granada, bitter over the government's dismissal of their followers. The Chamorro meeting was also under close scrutiny by the U.S. election board secretariat. Its proceedings were reported in the same manner as those of its counterpart in Managua. As expected, the former president effectively wielded his power, and this Conservative faction dutifully nominated the wealthy Rappaccioli.[49]

When the choice of both Conservative party candidates became official, the United States legation and national election board were faced with the unpleasant prospect of a three-man presidential contest. Since it was not likely that any one of these could obtain a majority, the final vote ultimately would have to be resolved in a Chamorro-run Congress — that is, if adherence to the Nicaraguan constitution were followed.[50]

McCoy was determined to save the supervision project. He announced to the national election board in June that he would give the two factions until July 28 to select one candidate. The general considered it better to have Carlos Cuadra Pasos, his personal choice for the Conservative nomination, step aside, along with the Chamorro candidate Rappaccioli, than to force a public showdown with the former president and probably lose.[51] McCoy announced that neither faction would be allowed to have its candidate placed on the ballot. As a follow-up to this decision, Ramon Castillo, the Conservative representative on the election board, was directed to inform his colleagues that unless they selected a compromise candidate by the stated deadline, the party label could not appear at polling stations in the general election. On the surface, this seemed like a minor restriction, but its enforcement would have meant almost certain defeat for the Conservatives. Illiterate voters were able to recognize a party only by the color of its insignia.[52]

General McCoy's action persuaded Carlos Cuadra Pasos

[48] Memorandum, Chamorro/Rappaccioli Convention, May 20, 1928, RG 43, Records, 1928 mission, folder P-2-A, NA.

[49] Ibid.

[50] National Election Board, confidential session, July 23, 1928, RG 43, Records, 1928 mission, folder B-5-D, NA.

[51] Ibid., confidential memorandum, July 28, 1928, RG 43, Records, 1928 mission, folder B-5-D, NA.

[52] Ibid., Election Board, confidential session, July 23, 1928.

to withdraw and seek a compromise candidate. Unquestionably, the board's decision to set a deadline indicated McCoy's determination to reject both Conservative candidates outright and end the party schism once and for all.

The general was not optimistic regarding prospects for a compromise between the two factions. He drew up a plan of his own whereby both the Díaz and Chamorro forces might agree on selecting a candidate. The framework within which both sides would negotiate established a 40-member Conservative general assembly, comprising the national directorates of the two groups. McCoy suggested Castillo be made chairman. Sessions would be held every day. All delegates would cast votes for candidates drawn from a list of 20 names, 10 selected by Chamorro and 10 chosen by Díaz.

General assembly proceedings took place in July and indicated beyond any doubt the deep personal divisions between the two groups and their leaders. While the meeting went through protracted debates, Díaz and Chamorro were convinced the split in the assembly could not provide the solution McCoy demanded. Ultimately, the two leaders would have to reach some agreement or be defeated by the Liberals in November, a prospect not entirely tragic for Chamorro.

While many believed Chamorro was indifferent to the need for nominating one Conservative candidate, the party *caudillo* knew that if the conservatives were denied a place on the ballot, congressional candidates might also be forced to submit to this party ban. The former president understood that his real strength lay in the legislature. He was far too astute a politician to risk losing this power base simply because he insisted on running his own presidential candidate, precluding any discussions with Díaz. Therefore, he and the president met in Managua on July 25 to reach a settlement.

Accounts of the meeting are not entirely clear. We know they discussed Chamorro's evident strength with the party's rank and file but not the manner in which the Conservative candidates were selected. Chamorro proved to be the better negotiator as his presidential nominee was accepted. Rappaccioli withdrew as the candidate, and the former president chose Adolfo Bénard, a wealthy sugar grower from Granada who openly favored U.S. policy in the country. To please the Díazistas, Julio Cardenal, a businessman from Managua, was selected as Bénard's running mate. Few doubt that Chamorro outmaneuvered Díaz in the secret conclave of July 25. The president failed to convince the others of his first choice or any other selection to head the ticket. When left to fend for himself, without assistance from U.S. diplomats, Díaz was no match for the intrepid Chamorro.[53]

The U.S. legation disliked the Bénard candidacy mainly because it was a Chamorro choice. Yet North American diplomats knew it would be difficult to reject him since he had been selected as the result of McCoy's direct order for negotiation. Observers surmised that the only hope preventing a Chamorro takeover if Bénard won was the candidate's wealth. McCoy staff members thought the wealthy conservative might exert more independence as a rich man who had never dabbled in politics and with no political obligations. The Conservative standard bearer's running mate, Julio Cardenal was Carlos Cuadra Pasos' brother in law. This choice obviously was considered a fortuitous one as he was sympathetic to the election supervision.[54]

As the campaign progressed, it became obvious that Bénard did not have the personality to attract a large following like Chamorro, nor did he possess the keen intellect of Cuadra Pasos. The Conservative standard bearer was a businessman who displayed little interest in politics. Chamorro's reason for supporting Bénard was simply the candidate's vast sum of money for a campaign. The *caudillo* of the Conservative forces knew full well his party was about to be placed at a disadvantage regarding the administration of the election itself. However, if a candidate with money could be nominated, a large propaganda campaign would offset the Conservative party's unfavorable position.[55]

Eberhardt and McCoy were pessimistic with respect to Bénard's chances for election. These feelings were based not so much on the candidate's apparent political ineptness but on the continuing split in local Conservative clubs. While McCoy's

---

[53] Julio Cardenal, interview with author, Managua, March 9, 1965. Cardenal said he was selected for this very reason. An interview with Chamorro confirmed this also. Managua, April 7, 1965.

[54] Eberhardt to State Department, August 4, 1928, RG 59, DF 817.00/5925, NA. The facts cited in this dispatch also were reported in Managua *La Noticia*, July 28, 1928, and corroborated by Cardenal in an interview with author (March 1965). He said, "Chamorro wanted `money bags' Bénard."

[55] Cardenal and Chamorro, interviews with author, Managua, April 1965.

ultimatum had forced a compromise on the warring Conservatives, it did not end Díaz' and Chamorro's deep antagonism. Chamorro was more concerned with the campaign to reelect his followers to Congress; Bénard had to please both groups and battle against a united Liberal party. The Conservative presidential candidate was to prove totally incapable of merging these two groups. His lack of political experience became more evident as the campaign progressed. Well before the election, McCoy was convinced Moncada would win handily the 1928 contest.[56]

Under Chamorro's leadership, the conservatives had to accept Bénard's candidacy, even though the latter was a political novice lacking the strength and stamina for a hard-fought campaign. Bénard himself said that the campaign was "...wasting my health and a tremendous sum of money in an occupation unsuited for me." While Chamorro had skillfully arranged for a candidate who had plenty of cash to finance a campaign, he did not select a man who could, in the opinion of many North Americans, effectively heal the Conservative party split.[57]

Third-Party Challengers: Liberal Republicans and Autonomist Nationalists

General McCoy believed Conservative party division and Sandino's military campaign were the foremost obstacles to his project of election supervision and installing a democratically elected chief executive. He also learned that the emergence of other political groups opposing the North American election project could become a critical problem. They were hoping to prevent an exclusively Liberal/ Conservative battle for the presidency. Above all, members of his staff, sympathetic to the Moncada candidacy, thought these elements could conceivably jeopardize chances for a Liberal victory.

Liberals had expressed concern in the spring of 1928 that parties once active in 1924 might reappear with the encouragement of the Conservative party. Additional political groups could take votes away from Liberals and deny their candidate the required majority for election. If this situation arose, Congress, as has already been noted, would have to determine the selection of a president. McCoy's earlier ultimatum to the

---

[56] Eberhardt to State Department, October 1, 1928, RG 59, DF 817.00/6044, NA.

[57] Ibid.

Conservatives had not ruled out the possibility of the legislature deciding the election's outcome. Consequently, the general became suspicious that Chamorro's effort to create a party split was closely tied with the emergence of splinter groups wanting to challenge the two-party system.[58]

At a diplomatic reception in the United States on April 4, César detailed the Conservatives' plan to have a third party established to draw votes from the Liberals.[59] He said Chamorro intended to encourage the reemergence of the Liberal Republican party led by Dr. Luis Felipe Corea, a former U.S. citizen and a 1924 presidential candidate. The Nicaraguan emissary said the new party would challenge regular Liberals' efforts to maintain a two-party contest. César correctly pointed out that in the 1924 campaign Dr. Corea had polled some seven thousand votes — less than 10 percent of the total vote. Therefore, if this margin were not changed appreciably in 1928, no candidate for the presidency would receive an electoral majority. Also, the minister confidently pointed out that Congress would select a chief executive in the end, precluding the U.S. supervision project from the election results.[60] This diplomatic indiscretion clearly indicated to the United States that the Conservatives would continue to try to prevent an electorate decision in the presidential race.[61]

The Liberal Republicans, more a personal following of Dr. Corea than a group with any special ideological base, announced in June they were entering their candidate in the presidential race. Congress, under Chamorro's direction, passed a resolution recognizing the presidential contender soon after the announcement. Chamorro's opinion about Corea's activities was obvious after this congressional action.[62]

In 1924, party leaders had spoken out against using U.S. election supervisors. Actually, they had never really made a

---

[58] Department of State to U.S. Legation, Managua, May 28, 1928, RG 59, DF 817.00/5704a, NA. Chamorro was aware of the significance these small parties could play denying the Conservative and Liberal presidential candidates and absolute majority. Interview with author, April 7, 1965.

[59] Memorandum of conversation, Stokely W. Morgan, chief, division of Latin American Affairs, April 4, 1928, RG 59, DF 817.00/5558, NA.

[60] Ibid.

[61] Chamorro, interview with author, April 7, 1965.

[62] *La Gaceta Oficial,* June 26, 1928.

concerted effort to support a candidate in the 1924 elections. In fact, at one point, they split with some supporting Liberals while others backed Conservatives. Moreover, a large number of Liberal Republicans came from the Conservative party. As the feud between Cuadra Pasos and the practical-minded Chamorro deepened in 1928, Corea hoped to be called upon as a compromise candidate. Now that the national election board had officially prevented the continuation of a Conservative party split, Chamorro hoped, at least, to add a third party in the contest.[63] Corea began a very active campaign with Chamorro's encouragement to adopt a platform almost solely dedicated to the withdrawal of General McCoy and his election supervisors. Moreover, the party attacked Moncada on one occasion as a "Liberal by conscience and not by deeds...a man who sold out his country's interests to further his own political ambitions."[64]

General McCoy then called upon Dr. Dodds, the architect of the 1924 Nicaraguan election law, to explain Corea's past activities and shed some light on dealing with third parties. Dodds reported to the election board chairman that Chamorro's ally had returned to Nicaragua in 1924 after a 17-year U.S. residence where he had become a citizen,[65] later renouncing it when the 1924 election got underway. Entering Nicaragua's race for the presidency, Dodds noted that he had received less than 10 percent of the vote that year. To McCoy's relief, this automatically disqualified the Liberal Republicans from continuing as a political party.[66]

On July 27, the party held its convention, and approximately one hundred delegates attended — all of whom supported Corea for personal rather than ideological reasons. However, the party conclave spent much of its time seeking names for a petition of official recognition rather than choosing candidates for public office. A Nicaraguan National Guard observer (a U.S. Marine officer) dispatched there reported that the Liberal Republicans were searching for ways in which the

---

63   Eberhardt to State Department, August 4, 1928, RG 59, DF 817.00/5919, NA. Chamorro, interview with author. Managua, April 7, 1965.

64   Managua *La Prensa*, July 31, 1928, 1.

65   Memorandum on Liberal Republican party, Harold W. Dodds, August 24, 1928, RG 43, Records, 1928 mission, folder P-5, NA.

66   Seven thousand votes were cast for Corea in 1924.

names Chamorro had gathered could be transferred to the Liberal Republican petition.[67]

The delegates welcomed people of all political persuasions who simply objected to the U.S. election supervision project. They also demanded Moncada be repudiated. Corea knew his chances for election were hopeless, yet he realized if enough votes were taken from Moncada, the Liberal party would be denied a chance of obtaining a majority in the general election.[68]

During this same period Toribio Tijerino, a former secretary and loyal stalwart of Chamorro, headed the Autonomist party. Like true Liberal Republicans, its members also condemned the marines and McCoy for interfering in the country's political affairs. To make matters more complicated, he publicly supported the Sandino cause and made use of the generally sympathetic Latin American press to popularize what he called "Nicaragua's second war for independence."

This was not Tijerino's debut in Nicaraguan politics. He had long since been an active, outspoken Chamorro supporter during the brief administration of Bartolomé Martínez (1923). He was made Nicaraguan consul general in New York and established numerous contacts with large financial interests in the United States. He ingratiated himself so well with Wall Street bankers that he was named to the National Bank of New York's board of directors at one point in his career. Through this position, at one point he managed to arrange for his country's re-purchase of a majority of shares in the republic's railroad.[69]

Tijerino's services in the Nicaraguan diplomatic corps and employment in New York did not deter him from taking an interest in the political affairs of his country. He found time to campaign for the coalition ticket headed by Conservative Carlos Solórzano in 1925. After this attempt to bring Liberals and Conservatives together failed, Tijerino became an ardent supporter of Juan Bautista Sacasa. The move from the Conservative to the Liberal party was apparently prompted by his

[67] Capt. General Víctor F. Bleasdale, assistant chief of staff, Intelligence, Nicaraguan National Guard, to McCoy, July 15, 1928, National Guard Intelligence Report, RG 43, Records, 1928 mission, folder P-5, NA.

[68] Ibid.

[69] Biography of Toribio Tijerino, Nicaraguan National Guard, RG 43, Records, 1928 mission, folder D-1-I.

disgust with the United States' choice of Adolfo Díaz for Nicaragua's chief executive in 1926.

As the 1927 civil war drew to a close and the United States brought the warring parties to the peace table, Sacasa left the country for Costa Rica, rejecting outright the United States' interventionist policy. The Liberal party was therefore split. Consequently, Tijerino hoped to fill a political void left by the departed Sacasa. He also backed the Sandino movement as the last line of defense within Nicaragua in the face of U.S. military action.[70]

The North American legation viewed the activities of Tijerino's party, the Autonomist Nationalists, as potentially dangerous to election supervision. It appealed to the patriotism of many people who admired but did not participate in Sandino's war against the North Americans. In any case, Washington's diplomats in Managua and members of McCoy's staff, not knowing how to deal with these splinter groups, concluded it was unwise to suppress Tijerino's activities.

Chamorro was as pleased with the emergence of Tijerino's Autonomist Nationalists as the United States legation was afraid of it.[71] In the Conservative leader's opinion, the Liberal Republicans acted merely as a dissident element in one major political party opposed to Moncada, whereas the Autonomist Nationalists called upon all political persuasions to resist U.S. intervention militarily and politically. Actually, it made little difference to Chamorro whether his party members joined either Corea or Tijerino. If Moncada or Bénard failed in their bids to obtain a majority of votes cast, the Chamorro-dominated Congress would decide the election anyway.[72]

In the early months of 1928, Tijerino began a speaking tour in the United States where he attacked the Coolidge administration for imposing a protectorate over his country and the marines for being unfit to be civics teachers. North American press gave his campaign of opposing military intervention and the electoral program considerable attention. He succeeded in enlisting support from numerous groups

---

[70] Managua *La Tribuna*, August 8, 1928, 1.

[71] Eberhardt to State Department, May 30, 1928, RG 59, DF 817.00/5709, NA. Tijerino later wrote of his great esteem for Chamorro. Toribio Tijerino, "Cartas Autoretrato, Mi Pelea," *Revista Conservadora de Pensamiento Centroamericano* (July 1962): 2. Chamorro, interview with author, Managua, April 7, 1965.

[72] Chamorro, interview with author, April 7, 1965.

which opposed Coolidge's Central American policy. It was believed that Tijerino was financed by the Anti-Imperialist League, an affiliate of the South American Bureau of the Comintern organized to pressure the U.S. government to withdraw all political and economic interests from Central America, especially Nicaragua.[73] Fortunately for Secretary of State Frank Kellogg, the 1928 Hoover/Smith campaign focused more on domestic problems than Tijerino's cries for removing marines from Nicaragua. Consequently, not gaining enough attention on his speaking tour, Tijerino returned to Nicaragua seeking funds from Conservatives to replenish his party's treasury. The party leader remained in Nicaragua only a short while as he failed to organize a strong active following. His plans for enlarging the Autonomist Nationalist party simply did not materialize on his return home.

Possibly, his party might well have acquired a number of disenchanted Conservatives had he been politicking in Nicaragua. However, by the time he returned to Managua, the two major parties had resolved their internal differences, nominated candidates, and set out to capture the presidency. By autumn, most Liberals and Conservatives were no longer interested in blocking McCoy's project by forming a third group. As a result, Tijerino found that time had run out. It was much too late to attract new members and offer a responsible program to the people in place of the Liberal and Conservative platforms. But his movement is significant because it represented a segment of Nicaraguan opinion that wanted total independence from Washington both militarily and politically.

The Liberals had long since selected a presidential candidate and felt confident as early as June that they had chosen the strongest presidential contender in Nicaragua. Furthermore, the party was convinced U.S. election supervisors were about to remove most of Díaz's executive powers during the election. Tijerino found it difficult to persuade his followers that success at the polls lay with the Autonomist Nationalist party, precluding a definitive victory by either of the two major candidates but likely to leave final power with Chamorro.

Tijerino also learned how difficult it was to raise money, as the Autonomist Nationalist had expected assistance from the Bénard following.[74] In fact, this was one of Tijerino's reasons

---

[73] Nicaraguan National Guard, intelligence report, September 24, 1928, RG 43, folder P-1-A.

for returning home. He learned that the Conservatives, especially the backers of the party's presidential candidate, did not want to support a group which could not possibly win. Actually, the most a well financed Autonomist Nationalist party could do was to prevent both major candidates from gaining a majority. Bénard was frankly reluctant to waste money on a group which would ultimately help Chamorro politically and not his own presidential efforts.[75] Tijerino concluded that his party could not gather the support needed to conduct an effective anti-U.S. campaign. In mid-summer, he returned to the United States to resume his anti-North American propaganda campaign and establish a permanent residence in New York City.[76]

Both the Autonomist Nationalists and the Liberal Republicans posed serious problems in a two-party presidential contest. McCoy wanted to prevent a congressional decision on the election's final outcome. Tijerino's departure happily solved part of the dilemma, leaving the Liberal Republicans, who, according to unofficial reports, had enlisted the support of approximately ten thousand people. McCoy took a calculated risk and decided that unless a party had submitted either a petition to qualify as a political group or nominated its candidates by March 1928, it could not appear on the ballot.[77] Fortunately, no one objected to this decision as leaders of both the Liberal and Conservative parties, with the exception of Chamorro, concluded nothing was to be gained financially or politically by using splinter group tactics.

---

[74] Ibid., July 12, 1928, RG 43, Records, 1928 mission, folder P-1-A, NA.

[75] Cardenal, interview with author, April 5, 1965.

[76] Department of Justice, Immigration and Naturalization Service, Central Files, 1923-1929.

[77] Nicaraguan National Guard, confidential intelligence report, July 29 to August 4, 1928, RG 43, Records, 1928 mission, folder M-10-A, NA.

President Adolfo Díaz.

U.S. Marines disarm first rebel in Nicaragua. (right)

LEÓN, NICARAGUA. (1927) Rebels turn in their arms to U.S. Marines in exchange for food and clothing. (below)

TIPITAPA, NICARAGUA. U.S. Marines issue food and clothing to disarmed soldiers.

U.S. Marines observe an election banner in Nicaragua (1928).

President José Maria Moncada in Nicaragua,
circa 1927-1928.

VI

Peacefully Voting: From San Juan del Sur to Ocotal and Talpaneca

THE PRESIDENCY: Power Reduced

During SUMMER AND AUTUMN of 1928, North American election supervisors, with a sense of urgency in all parts of Nicaragua, requested that steps be taken to reduce Díaz's power. Although Liberals appeared certain of victory, they were convinced the party would be successful only if the president were relieved of his executive authority altogether.[1] McCoy faced a dilemma as the electoral law had not given North American supervisors the right to impose direct restrictions on the Nicaraguan chief executive. However, a Liberal victory depended upon impartial handling of the election machinery, namely communications facilities, and proper utilization of public authority.

On October 24, an intelligence report came to the attention of General Elias Beadle, the North American director of the Nicaraguan National Guard. It stated that numerous clandestine meetings were being held by former high-ranking army officers who planned to instigate disturbances just before the election. If the Conservative administration were to succeed in retaining its vast police power, as it expected to do, chaos could be used as an excuse to keep the party in power by declaring a state of siege and martial law. Other communications corroborated the report; one from Carlos Cuadra Pasos told a National Guard commander that Díaz had decided to continue on as president after 1928 in light of the unstable political situation.[2]

---

[1] Col. Cornelius Smith, president, election board, Department of Granada, to McCoy, September 8, 1928, RG 43, Records, 1928 Electoral Mission, folder B-3-F, NA.

[2] Commander, Nicaraguan National Guard, Department of Granada, to Gen. Elias Beadle, commander, National Guard, October 24, 1928, RG 43, D-1-I, NA.

This revelation and numerous others like it convinced McCoy and his advisers that the president had to have his powers reduced and monitored. As reports of the large Liberal registration spread, Conservatives planned to use all kinds of tactics to prevent Moncada's election. The United States decided that its own military forces would be concentrated in the northern departments of Matagalpa, Jinotega, Estelí and Nueva Segovia under the North American-led Nicaraguan National Guard.

By August, the guard actually assumed a direct role in the anti-Sandino campaign over objections from the commander of the Second Marine Brigade. There was increasing friction between the regular Marine Brigade Commander Logan Feland and Elias Beadle, the marine who headed the guard or who would be deployed during the election.[3] On August 28, the president issued an executive decree prohibiting political groups from congregating without the express permission of local police authority. General Beadle took over law enforcement responsibilities and jointly, with Díaz, ordered all groups to secure a license from the marine general to hold political rallies. They believed these orders would reduce, if not altogether obviate, Conservative attempts to arouse undue confusion on or before election day. This decision actually deepened the friction between the two senior North American military officers, Beadle and Feland, over the deployment of their respective military commands, the regular marine force, and the U.S.-commanded Nicaraguan National Guard.

In September, National Guardsmen were preventing *alcaldes* (mayors) in towns and cities from participating in political activities. North American national election board members considered this action too extreme. They objected to Beadle's actions regarding the removal of police power from local law enforcement officers and pointed out that the electoral decree never gave General McCoy or Beadle such power.[4]

The ban on political rallies clearly indicated that the president had agreed (willingly or unwillingly) to Beadle's plan for assuming police authority. The significance of using the guard rather than the marines was best expressed by U.S.

---

[3] Elias Beadle, General Order 28, August 25, 1928, Headquarters, National Guard, RG 43, folder 0-2-G, NA.

[4] Dodds to McCoy, September 29, 1928, RG 43, Records, 1928 mission, folder I-5-D, NA.

Chargé Dana Munro, who wrote to Assistant Secretary of State
Francis White, "The National Guard is an instrument of the State
Department's policy here, and everything affecting its organization and its efficiency is of the utmost importance to us."[5] A
tremendous amount of Díaz's authority had been removed,
and the Liberals acknowledged a significant step had been
taken in the election supervision project.

Nicaraguan citizens who did not accept the idea of a non-
political army viewed skeptically the police authority assumed
by the Nicaraguan National Guard under North American
command. To minimize the possibility of misusing this newly
acquired authority, General Elias Beadle decided to eliminate
well-known and suspected undesirables in his "army." People
were reporting unfair and even blatant misuse of National
Guard soldiers' power. Consequently, the general gathered a
number of these "potential instigators" and created what he
called a "replacement company" and assigned it to the national
penitentiary for patrol duty.[6]

General McCoy approved the move, and the election
board noted that complaints declined rapidly as voting day
approached. The purge within the North American-led National Guard went largely unnoticed. Its success clearly points
out the tremendous power vested in McCoy as the Nicaraguan
government was not notified of the operation.[7]

U.S. staff members of the national election board were not
satisfied that sufficient control had been established over the
country by autumn 1928. McCoy had not, as yet, exerted
supervision or control over locating where votes would be
reported and tabulated in the communication system. During
the summer of 1928, his staff members wanted telephone,
radio, and telegraph operations removed from the government
before the Liberals objected to the management of these
facilities by their opposition. Major Cassius W. Dowell, of
McCoy's staff, urged that "suggestions be made to the chief
executive for having three marines assigned to the national
communications office and assist him [Díaz] in giving proper

---

[5] Munro to White, November 3, 1928, Diplomatic Records,
Department of State, hereinafter cited as RG 59, DF 817.00/1051/234,
NA.

[6] Beadle to McCoy, confidential memorandum, August 17, 1928,
RG 43, Records, 1928 mission, folder G-15, NA.

[7] Munro to White, November 3, 1928, RG 59, DF 817.00/1051/234,
NA.

supervision."[8]   This was a compromise. The president could leave his appointee in, and McCoy would have observers stationed there to see that no irregularities took place during the election.

Díaz ordered his director of communications to revamp the operating procedures of the country's telephone, telegraph, and radio systems, "on the basis of [the] recommendation made by General McCoy's election board."[9] Even though the North American general had his way this time, the Liberal campaign to have him exert more direct control over all departmental communications offices continued.[10] In fact, election board chairmen throughout the country reported Conservatives were still in full control of communication centers. The chief complaint was that Liberals were finding it almost impossible to send messages to their party offices in Managua.[11]

There were congressional elections to be contested in 1928, too. Chamorro decided to concentrate on them and maintain his power in the national legislature. If the Conservative party could do this, final canvassing and vote tabulation might delay the inauguration of a new chief executive. Or better, should either Moncada or Bénard fail to gain an absolute majority, Congress would elect a president. Chamorro was convinced Conservative representation could be increased in the Senate and Chamber of Deputies in the congressional contests. He reaffirmed this later on by stating, "I expected to make full use of the congressional election in the 1928 presidential races."[12]

The United States-run national election board knew the Liberals held a wide margin in voter registration in most departments. McCoy wanted this kept as quiet as possible to minimize Chamorro's perceived efforts to obstruct the election

[8] Maj. Cassius M. Dowell, executive officer, office of the secretariat, U.S. electoral mission staff, to McCoy, August 3, 1928, RG 43, Records, 1928 mission, folder C-16, NA.

[9] Antonio Gúzman, *Memorias* (Managua: Imprenta Nacional, 1928), 32.

[10] President, election board, Jinotega, to McCoy, September 28, 1928, RG 43, Records, 1928 mission, folder C-15-B, NA.

[11] Ibid.

[12] Chamorro, interview with author, Managua, April 7, 1965

proceedings.[13] Moncada was aware the 1928 electoral law did not provide for U.S. supervision of the congressional elections. If involvement in them took place, it would pose a very delicate problem for McCoy and his staff. However, if the issue were neglected, the objectives of the supervised presidential election could be destroyed altogether.

Five vancancies occurred in the Nicaraguan Senate during spring and summer of 1928 due to deaths and resignations. The constitution stipulated the president of the republic would "take the necessary action to fill the seat not later than one month after the vacancy occurred."[14] Members of McCoy's staff thought these openings could easily be filled during the regular presidential election.

Moncada was particularly anxious to have the five Senate seats contested. He realized if all were elected as Liberals this would give his party at least the same number of places in the Senate as the Conservatives. Success in all these contests would at least have created a deadlock in the Congress if Chamorro insisted on canvassing the votes after the election.

Díaz delayed making the appointments since they were in the predominantly Liberal departments of Estelí, Nueva Segovia, Condoles, and Matagalpa. McCoy, fearful of the consequences should this congressional issue go unattended, decided to act. He expressed displeasure to the president and reminded him the constitution required prompt action in appointing or arranging for election to the national Congress.[15] Yet Díaz refused to move on the issue, and this caused the North American supervisor to be suspicious. Consequently, he decided to maintain an unofficial but continued interest in the senatorial and congressional contests. When the minister of government was asked for a complete list of congressional nominees, McCoy found, to his dismay, that the names of many candidates had been left off. Predictably, these were members of the Liberal party. Furthermore, the five names omitted came from safe Liberal districts where Moncada had expected to elect Liberals to balance Senate membership.[16]

---

[13] Nicaraguan National Guard to McCoy, intelligence report, October 3, 1928, RG 43, Records, 1928 mission, folder 0-4, NA.

[14] Ibid.

[15] Letter, McCoy to President Díaz, August 22, 1928, RG 43, Records, 1928 mission, folder V-5, NA, Photocopy.

[16] Memorandum, Senate races, U.S. electoral mission staff, n.d., RG 43, Records, 1928 mission, folder 0-4-A, NA.

The national election board then undertook a complete and detailed study, examining the qualifications of the congressional candidates. The Liberals were encouraged when they learned that McCoy insisted these contests be held concurrently with the presidential election and not filled by executive appointment. Díaz did not realize McCoy had already decided to have all the votes canvassed in congressional contests as well. Moreover, the chairman also had directed the national election board to prepare certificates legalizing the congressional elections when they took place on the day of the presidential contest.[17]

The Request for Continued Election Supervision

A few weeks before the 1928 election, the State Department decided, that to insure continued stability of Nicaragua's constitutional government and provide a framework for electoral proceedings, the marines might have to remain there indefinitely. This decision was not revealed publicly of course, especially during the 1928 Hoover/Smith presidential campaign. U.S. officials were convinced that the Liberals had received an opportunity to compete on an equal basis with the Conservatives and that the same condition would have to be created for the Díaz party if it lost.[18]

This policy decision had some interesting implications. The United States was convinced well before the Nicaraguan presidential election that it would be dealing with a new party in power and one which segments had opposed U.S. military and political intervention. Therefore, a continued close watch on Nicaragua's politics beyond 1928 was contemplated. Moreover, throughout the presidential campaign, Moncada was confident he would defeat Bénard handily. With this in mind, the Liberal standard bearer began to think of problems he would face as the new president. He knew Augusto César Sandino would not accept his election. And since the National Guard had not been built up to full strength, how could he then

---

[17] G.W. Brown, legal staff, U.S. electoral mission, to Minister, Gobernación, August 28, 1928, RG 43, Records, 1928 mission, folder 0-4-A, NA, Photocopy.

[18] Memorandum, Department of State, RG 59, DF 817.00/6026, NA. See also Secretary of State Kellogg to U.S. legation, Managua, October 3, 1928, RG 59, DF 817.00/6007, NA.

expect to establish domestic peace and end the guerrillas' campaign?[19] In October, Moncada met with Admiral David F. Sellers, commander of the U.S. Special Service Squadron in Nicaragua, to discuss the situation. He asked the marines to remain in the republic at least until the National Guard (constabulary) could be built up to full strength.[20]

When the leading candidate and probable winner of the presidential contest in 1928 looked favorably on continued military occupation, prospects for another supervised election seemed good. If the next Nicaraguan president wanted U.S. help in preserving political stability through election supervision, the State Department was prepared to provide it.

Moncada's appeal encouraged the North American legation in Managua to arrange some sort of public request by both candidates urging subsequent supervised elections. When the Liberal candidate expressed his willingness to retain the marines, the State Department, anxious to strengthen the guard and insure a stable political structure, decided to secure an agreement between the two major parties. Eberhardt best expressed the legation's feeling when he said, "Little of permanent value will be gained by holding a free election now [1928] if the defeated party feels that future elections will be dominated by the administration, and that it therefore has no hope of subsequently attaining power except by violence."[21]

Eberhardt's observations implied that the Conservatives might lose in 1928 and subsequently need some kind of protection from the arbitrary and possibly capricious Liberal administration to take over. He thought the pending change in governments made it necessary for the United States "...to exercise a powerful influence with the discontented elements for the maintenance of peace and thereby supervise the 1930 and 1932 elections."[22]

A cabinet meeting was held at the White House on October 5, 1928, to discuss continued military occupation in

---

[19] José M. Moncada, *Estados Unidos en Nicaragua*, (Managua: Tipografia Atenas, 1942), 21.

[20] Adm. D.F. Sellers, commander, Special Service Squadron, to U.S. Chief of Naval Operations (copy), n.d., RG 59, DF 817.00/616, NA.

[21] Eberhardt to State Department, October 1, 1928, RG 59, DF 817.00/6007, NA. See also Kellogg to Eberhardt, February 15, 1929, RG 59, DF 817.00/-1051/245, NA.

[22] Ibid.

Nicaragua. Assistant Secretary of State Francis White urged President Coolidge to keep the marines in the republic to prevent the defeated party from hindering the elected president. Coolidge accepted White's proposal and agreed not to reduce the number of troops immediately after November 4th, election day.[23]

An important decision had therefore been made regarding the North American presence in Nicaragua. However, the secretary of state was particularly anxious that Eberhardt and McCoy not become directly involved planning alone future election supervision commitments. Kellogg thought it would be far better to have Moncada and Bénard exchange letters, each pledging to support supervised elections in 1930 and 1932.[24]

The legation proceeded to carry out Kellogg's directive, and Moncada was advised of this tactic. Shortly thereafter, he and Bénard agreed to more supervised elections. Apparently, a verbal agreement was not enough. The U.S. legation wrote a draft of Moncada's letter for him. The final product addressed to the Conservative standard bearer betrays much of the select wording which was included in the original letter.[25] Furthermore, they decided the Moncada/Bénard correspondence would not be released until it was certain the Conservative leader would accept the proposal. By this time, Bénard and his running mate were convinced that their only chance for preventing the Liberals from misusing their expected new authority was to have the United States continue running the election machinery.[26]

Bénard promptly accepted Moncada's proposal, and both men publicly exchanged their letters pledging to support outside supervision of the 1930 and 1932 congressional and

---

[23] Memorandum, cabinet meeting, October 5, 1928, RG 59, DF 817.00/6026, NA. Actually, in early 1929, the number of marines was reduced from 5,000 to 3,500 and by late autumn 1929, to 1,800. This was done at a time when Stimson, Kellogg's successor, wanted the National Guard to pacify the disrupted northern department rather than continue the program the marines conducted. By January 1931, the marine force was reduced further to 1,412 personnel.

[24] Kellogg to U.S. legation, Managua, October 3, 1928, RG 59, DF 817.00/6007, NA.

[25] The 1932 Election Supervision Agreement, October 30, 1928, RG 43, Records, 1928 mission, folder D-5-A, NA.

[26] Julio Cardenal, interview with author, Managua, March 30, 1965.

presidential elections. The Conservative candidate was clearly more effusive in his praise for the United States and understandably so if defeat was in the offing. Bénard wrote his opponent, "The [North] American supervision has come to give us the enjoyment of election freedom which will bring a long era of national tranquility to the welfare of all, Liberals as well as Conservatives.[27]

Even though Liberals and Conservatives accepted McCoy's supervisory role, the United States wanted the candidates to understand fully the nature of North American intervention in the future. So, just before the election, in a letter to both presidential contenders, General Elias Beadle conveyed U.S. intentions more candidly and forcefully:

> With a view of carrying in full the provisions of the Stimson Agreement, a pact between the contending political parties of Nicaragua and the government of the United States....the president of the United States assures Nicaragua that the military and naval forces of the United States...will remain in Nicaragua to insure the inauguration of the president elected on November 4, 1928, and the firm establishment of his government and for such further period of time as may be necessary for the newly reorganized Nicaraguan National Guard to demonstrate clearly its ability to preserve peace and order.[28]

As election day approached, none of the two parties' leaders doubted U.S. intentions to maintain a close watch over Nicaraguan political developments. The first step in the election supervision was about to take place. McCoy's election board initiated a plan to provide maximum security for voters. All of the approximately 5,000 U.S. military personnel patrolled roads and areas near voting booths. Many marine officers and enlisted personnel in administrative and noncombat positions were dispatched to field commands, such as Liberal strongholds in Nueva Segovia, Jinotega, Matagalpa, and Chontales.

---

[27] Adolfo Bénard to Moncada, n.d., RG 43, Records, 1928 mission, folder B-5-A, NA, Photocopy.

[28] Beadle to Bénard and Moncada (copy), n.d., RG 43, Records, 1928 mission, folder B-5-A, NA.

A compilation of registered voters indicated that the Liberals were clearly outnumbering the Conservatives by a substantial margin. In fact, local election board supervisors and the national election board were convinced that if proper safeguards could be set up, the Liberals would easily win the election. However, Sandino was prepared to disrupt the election if possible.

The increased number of raids, some under the leadership of a Sandino cohort, Pedro Altamirano in Jinotega, coincided with the release of these reports showing a large Liberal registration. General McCoy then instituted what seems to have been a major step to increase prospects for peace in the northern department. His plan was to offer Sandino amnesty if the rebel bands ceased their hit-and-run tactics and intimidation. All department chairmen were instructed to be ready for any signs of Sandino's accepting an offer to negotiate.

Sandino's confidence was reinforced when he heard the offer. It appeared to him the U.S. was "desperate" to end "election board harassment." Many rebels were pleased at the overture as it seemed to show that the marines were finally admitting defeat in the guerrilla war. In any case, they never considered accepting the McCoy offer. Instead, the Sandinistas became more confident and determined to disrupt the election proceedings. Later in January 1929, Sandino offered to meet President-elect Moncada, but the new chief executive rejected the offer.[29]

On November 4, 1928, Nicaragua marked an end to a segment of its political history. The Liberal party, which had opposed U.S. intervention and had been out of power since 1909, confidently named Moncada as its candidate for president under the aegis of a U.S.-supervised election project. As marine patrols guarded the paths and dirt roads in areas of the Sandino-held north, combat-ready troops remained at discreet distances from the polling booths in the more settled regions of the south. A North American officer working on the supervision program conveyed an interesting portrayal of the day's activities when he recorded these impressions:

> Sunday, election day, started just as every other Sunday had started in Nicaragua, clanging church bells started slowly and ended with a terrible air and

---

[29] U.S. Marine Corps, 11th Regiment, intelligence report, November 18, 1928, RG 43, Records, 1928 mission, folder R-2, NA.

a sudden noiseless stop. Chorus of roosters. A symphony of bird sounds. Dull and sullen skies above and dirty dust below. Trucks rattled along the streets. The dull *moyo* led plodding bullocks along with his sharp-pointed stick resting on the yoke behind. Trumpets of reveille awakened marines all over Nicaragua — about eighty garrisons of them from Greytown to Cape Gracias a Dios, from San Juan del Sur to Ocotal and Telpaneca — 5,642 officers and men of the navy and marines and 1,869 National Guard. The Nicaraguans peacefully voted and "dipped their fingers" in the red stain to indicate that they had voted once. It had been said that Adolfo Díaz, being president, would not "dip his finger." A marine officer, desiring an official picture of the president "dipping his finger" requested him to do so. He acquiesced gladly and the picture was taken. The news spread rapidly, and the incident had a very beneficial effect on some Nicaraguans who had declared that they would not vote because they considered themselves equal to the president. Propaganda was rampant, including stories spread by Sandino among the Indians, that the North Americans would use a chemical to poison the voters.

When the ballots and election records from the voting places arrived at the departmental capitols [sic], guards of marines were placed over them until they were taken to Managua under escort. The marines brought in the ballot boxes from all over Nicaragua on mules, bull carts, pack bulls, air-planes, ...boats on Lakes Nicaragua and Managua, attainable trucks, and on their shoulders.[30]

By election day at noon, most of the registered voters had cast their ballots in three quarters of the departments. As marines and guardsmen patrolled the telephone and telegraph lines, returns were sent to McCoy quickly and without interruption.

---

[30] Edward McClellan, "Supervising the Nicaraguan Election," *United States Naval Institutional Proceedings* 59: 1 (January 1933): 38.

José Maria Moncada received 76,676 votes to 56,987 for Adolfo Bénard. This gave the Liberal party a 19,689 vote margin out of a total of 133,663 votes cast. Ninety percent of those who had registered in September and October cast a ballot on election day.[31] Fifty thousand more people voted in 1928 than in 1924. While the percentage of citizens voting in 1928 appears to have been suspiciously high, both parties accepted it as accurate.[32]

Many factors accounted for the decisive Conservative defeat; foremost among them was Bénard's ineptness as a political leader. He had never been tested as a political leader. Furthermore, he demonstrated a defeatist attitude throughout the entire election period. His running mate, Julio Cardenal, was absolutely convinced that the United States was working for Moncada's election and, as a result, did not feel the full effort of a campaign should be undertaken.[33] How then could the party expect to hope for victory or work hard to achieve it, if its leaders showed no enthusiasm or confidence? Certainly, the Chamorro/Díaz split did not help to solidify the party, and the compromise did nothing to heal its wounds by election time either. As a result, Chamorristas failed to work for Bénard.

The Conservatives had been in power for 18 years. It was now particularly difficult for Adolfo Díaz to defend his party's many abuses or to justify the policies of a group which had ruled Nicaragua for so long. The Coolidge government had been actively interested in creating Nicaraguan political stability with minimal military intervention, leaving power to an incumbent regime. Election supervision had forced the Conservatives to compete for votes on an equal basis with their opponents. Police control and supervision of the numerous government revenue-producing institutions denied the Díaz government funds to pay its workers for support. As a result, large segments of this group who might have remained loyal switched to the Liberal party in the last few weeks of the campaign.[34]

---

[31] Eberhardt to State Department, October 16, 1928, RG 43, Records, 1928 mission, folder M-10-H, NA, Photocopy.

[32] Figures compiled by Liberal and Conservative party members of the election board were the same as those drawn up by McCoy's staff. Total registration was 148,831.

[33] Cardenal, interview with author, Managua, March 30, 1965.

[34] Harold W. Dodds, "American Supervision of Nicaraguan Election," *Foreign Affairs* 7 (April 1929): 494.

Conservative party members conceded defeat and made no effort to object to or negate the final figure in the votes cast. The leading party paper summarized the new attitude of the Conservatives when it said:

> We must frankly admit the victory of our political adversaries. With unrestricted freedom the Nicaraguan citizens went to the polls under [North] American supervision. Conservatives and Liberals made use of their right to vote. The Liberals obtained the victory in a democratic struggle.

> We who know the root causes of the Conservative defeat are not going to sit down by the roadside and cry over our misfortunes, neither are we going to charge election frauds. [North] American honesty in the supervision of the election must constitute a testimonial and a cause of legitimate pride.[35]

The Conservative party was faced with the prospect of being the out party. Its only hope for regaining control was by relying on the good offices and U.S. influence in the future. Therefore, the outward display of editorial praise for General Frank Ross McCoy would certainly do no harm. This was to be especially beneficial as the Conservatives, in turn, launched a new era of cooperation with the United States.

An accurate indication that the party was about to depart from its policy of "obstructionism" was evident in Chamorro's activities. He still retained great influence in the Senate and Chamber of Deputies. The bill establishing the National Guard, which was introduced in December 1927, was finally approved by the Nicaraguan Congress in January 1929, and the United States took note of Chamorro's efforts to secure its passage.[36] Up to this time, the Conservative *caudillo* had managed to embarrass Washington by not supporting the creation of a National Guard and proposing an election law. Conservative party tactics after the 1928 election changed noticeably. There were three significant outcomes from the contest: the victory of the pro-election supervision project wing of the Liberal

---

[35] Managua *La Prensa*, November 7, 1928, 1.

[36] Eberhardt to State Department, December 3, 1928, RG 59, DF 811.00/6138, NA.

party; Liberal Sandino's continuation of a campaign to oust U.S. Marines from the country; and, for the first time in Nicaraguan history, an executive power transferred from one party to another with both presidential candidates present at an inauguration.

VII

Monitoring and Watching the Conduct of Democracy: The 1930 Congressional and 1931 Municipal Elections

The Dispatch of an Election Board Chairman

THREE DAYS AFTER President Moncada took office in January 1929, U.S. Minister Charles Eberhardt had a private conversation with the new chief executive in which they discussed prospects for appointing a permanent election supervisor.[1] The U.S. legation was somewhat encouraged by Moncada's continued willingness to abide by the 1927 Tipitapa agreement. Certainly, this was a good omen. It was also reported, albeit incorrectly, that Sandino had left for Mexico. He would leave Nicaragua later in May 1929. In any case, this news created a widespread feeling of relief, especially in the White House and State Department.[2] Problems for supervising future elections seemed remote at the dawn of 1929 since the new president appeared willing to cooperate fully with the Hoover administration.

On February 12, 1929, Moncada's foreign minister asked the United States to consider supervising Nicaraguan elections for "supreme authorities" again. The State Department quickly accepted this dispatch as a formal request to supervise all political contests up to and including the 1932 presidential

---

[1] As reported by new U.S. Minister Matthew Hanna, Managua, January 4, 1929, to State Department, RG 59, DF 817.00/6166, NA.

[2] Munro to State Department, February 21, 1929, RG 59, DF 817.00/43, NA. Sandino left Nicaragua in June 1929 and returned to his country in May 1930. His departure in 1929 was facilitated by the United States.

race. The United States thought this was an extremely valuable document as it committed the Liberals to accept a U.S.-supervised election while plans were made to reduce the marine contingent. As later events were to show, President Moncada did not interpret the request in this manner. In any case, relations with the Hoover administration got off to a good start, even though the meaning of the February communication was vague.[3]

In his first message to Congress in December 1929, President Herbert Hoover reported he had already withdrawn a third of the U.S. Marines from Nicaragua, leaving a total of 1,800. The chief executive further stated he was determined to evacuate the remaining 1,800 soon.[4] This was a major step in the new administration's policy of ending armed U.S. intervention in Latin America. In autumn of 1928, approximately five thousand men had been on duty in the republic. In his memoirs, Stimson recalls that troop reduction was the beginning of a policy of "deliberate non-interference in Central America."[5] The planned withdrawal of U.S. armed forces in Nicaragua was undoubtedly a notable goal. But the United States' continued involvement in internal affairs of this Central American republic through election supervision was to continue even though direct military intervention was winding down.

In February 1930, Díaz and Chamorro reported to the United States legation that President Moncada planned to cancel the 1932 election and extend his term for an additional four years. This was particularly disturbing to Stimson, now Secretary of State, as he respected the president and held him in high esteem. A development of this kind, if true, would obviously mar their good personal relations.[6] The two former presidents were unable to produce evidence to substantiate their charge, but they warned the United States that a Liberal

---

[3] Foreign Minister of Nicaragua to the State Department, February 12, 1929, RG 59, DF 817.00/110, NA.

[4] William S. Myers, ed., *The State Papers and Other Public Writings of Herbert Hoover,* (Garden City, New York: Doubleday, Doran & Co., 1934), 1:140. In January 1929, there were more than 5,000 marines. By July of the same year, the number was reduced to 2,500 and then to 1,412 by the end of the year.

[5] Stimson and Bundy, *On Active Service,* 156.

[6] Willard Beaulac, Chargé d'Affaires, Managua, to State Department, February 27, 1930, RG 59, DF 817.00/6550, NA.

member in the Chamber of Deputies would soon offer a proposal suggesting the cancellation of elections and continuing Moncada's term of office. The State Department wanted to make sure this legislative maneuver did not take place. It directed the legation to inform the Nicaraguan government immediately that such a scheme would be "especially unwelcome to the government of the United States."[7]

Díaz's and Chamorro's warnings regrettably proved correct. The United States' views as expressed to Moncada had no effect on the Liberal administration. On March 15, a Liberal senator introduced a bill which stipulated that the president could arbitrarily extend his term of office if military disturbances, presumably Sandino's guerrilla campaign, did not subside. This was actually becoming a dangerous problem again in 1930. Even the U.S. legation admitted it was reaching a critical stage in its relations with the Nicaraguan president.[8] Many Liberal partisans of the chief executive believed he would need vast powers to cope with this problem and thereby forego, as one ally said, "the distractions of an election."[9] The United States had to face the dual threat of Sandino's continued operations and a political crisis, namely an extended presidential term.

Moncada was proving difficult in other respects too. The Department of State wanted the National Guard strengthened to deemphasize marine activities and suggested reducing appropriations for it. Moncada objected, claiming the proposed cutbacks would comprise almost 25 percent of his budget. The chief executive finally approved $854,000, far below the figure recommended by the North American National Guard commander, Colonel Douglas McDougal. Budget constraints had actually reduced the size of the guard from 2,256 to 1,810 by December 1930. Washington insisted that enlisted men and officers, numbering a little over one thousand, be sent to areas where Augusto Sandino forces were holding territory.

The State Department was unable to find evidence implicating Moncada in a move to extend his presidential term. In any case, the United States was concerned that if the

---

[7] State Department to the legation, Managua, March 15, 1930, RG 59, DF 817.00/6555, NA.

[8] Hanna to State Department, May 27, 1930, RG 59, DF 817.00/6643, NA.

[9] Managua *La Gaceta Oficial*, March 13, 1930.

Nicaraguan Congress adopted the proposal, the 1932 supervision of elections would prove difficult, if not altogether impossible. Consequently, the State Department's Latin American Affairs Division did not want to lose time in preparing for the 1930 congressional elections. If continued interest were to be maintained in Nicaragua's politics through the 1932 presidential race, an election board chairman was needed to oversee the 1930 congressional contests. They decided to send a supervisor in the spring of 1930, well in advance of the autumn campaigns.[10]

Former President Díaz was so alarmed over the prospects for an extension of Moncada's rule, he told Matthew Hanna, the new U.S. minister, that the Conservative party would not nominate congressional candidates unless the United States supervised the 1930 elections.[11] The former president and Nicaraguan conservative party press demanded the same restrictions be placed on the Liberals as had been imposed on them in 1928.[12]

Hanna prevailed upon the president to issue a decree announcing that the United States would run the 1930 elections. The North American diplomat's success in this regard was due in no small way to his developing a friendship with the Liberal president. Moncada's concurrence with Hanna's request pleased the legation, and the issue of *continuismo* ended for the time being. Hanna quickly asked Stimson to send the president a note publicly praising him for his decision. He was certain that flattering the vain chief executive would do a great deal of good, paving the way for autumn congressional elections.[13] Now that Moncada had promised to issue a decree calling for supervision of the congressional elections, the United States was confident that the presence of a U.S. election board chairman would hamper plans for the rumored extension of a presidential term in 1932.

Actually, the State Department decided not to wait for Moncada's request for an election supervisor. It selected Chief of Naval Intelligence Captain Alfred W. Johnson as the next chairman of the national election board. He was appointed

---

[10] Memorandum, commandant, U.S. Marine Corps to Chief of Naval Operations, April 18, 1930, RG 59, DF 817.00/6618, NA.

[11] Hanna to State Department, n.d., RG 59, DF 817.00/6618, NA.

[12] Managua *La Prensa*, May 8, 1930.

[13] Hanna to White, May 23, 1930, RG 59, DF 817.00/6645, NA.

primarily because he had not been associated previously with the occupation forces in Nicaragua, and the United States wanted a fresh start in the venture.[14]

Johnson had a long and very distinguished career in the navy. He fought in the Spanish-American War and shortly thereafter was assigned to the Asiatic Fleet during the Philippine insurrection in 1901-1902. He served as military attaché in Chile from 1911 to 1912. During World War I, he commanded the destroyer *Conyngham* in the first naval force to go overseas. At the end of the war he served in various assignments in Asia and finally became chief of naval intelligence in 1927.[15]

Johnson was by no means as adequately prepared for this new assignment as his predecessor McCoy. He was bright, competent, and aware of the political events in the republic from 1927 when he began his assignment as the navy's chief intelligence officer. However, he had none of the diplomatic skills essential for effective management of this mission.

The captain took over his post in May 1930 by studying the Dodds law of 1923, which went back into effect at the conclusion of the 1928 election. It provided that a Nicaraguan representing the party which gained the largest vote in the preceding election be chairman of the national election board. Moreover, all departmental board presidents would in turn be appointed by the national chairman. Stimson wanted the Dodds law amended again in such a way as to empower U.S. citizens to preside over all election boards. The secretary further stipulated that these supervisors should have a veto over both the Liberal and Conservative representatives.[16] Above all, Stimson was anxious that the Nicaraguan Congress not canvass the final vote tabulation as prescribed in Dodds' law. He wanted Johnson to carry this out just as McCoy had done in 1928, avoiding interference by a Chamorro-dominated Chamber of Deputies.[17]

When the North American navy captain reached Managua

---

[14] Ibid.

[15] *Officer Biographies,* Operational Archives, Naval Historical Center, Department of Navy, Washington, D.C.

[16] Memorandum on elections, Johnson electoral mission, June 10, 1930, RG 59, DF 817.00/38, NA. Portions of the 1930 election mission documents are incorporated with State Department Records.

[17] Ibid.

in July 1930, Moncada informed him that he would not submit the proposed revised law to the legislature. The president said that Supreme Court members had warned him they would rule it unconstitutional. Johnson agreed it was far better and safer to issue the new law as an executive decree as McCoy had done in 1928. Stimson's concern that Congress still posed formidable obstacles to an amended law were well founded. He was thankful Moncada took his advice and understood the problem too. Obviously, the Stimson/Moncada friendship, cordial and warm, was still critically important to the election supervision project.[18]

Johnson was joined by 13 U.S. Army officers, all of whom had served under General Frank McCoy in 1928. Their continued service was a wise move as these men were thoroughly familiar with the political conditions in the country. However, they were finding the Liberals more intractable and difficult to deal with compared to the Conservatives in 1928.[19]

Now that Stimson had managed to have Johnson accepted as the national election board chairman, he moved to solidify his strategy regarding election supervision through 1932. He wanted the Nicaraguan president's request in writing for supervision in 1930 to include the 1932 contest as well. Stimson's instructions to the captain removed all doubt as to the reason for the latter's mission and its significance for the 1932 presidential race. Johnson's orders, lengthy and verbose, were to "carry on to a further point of advancement the cooperation of this government in electoral matters which has extended during the presidential elections of 1928...[to] be extended in connection with the impending congressional elections and later the presidential elections." Put simply, it meant "get an approval for running the 1932 election." The secretary of state was hopeful that the ambiguities of the Tipitapa understanding finally had been clarified in this directive to the North American election board chairman.[20]

After Captain Johnson reached Nicaragua in July 1930, Sandino personally led military operations in Jinotega. Undoubtedly, prospects for another period of interference by the U.S. government contributed in large part to the resurgent rebel

---

[18] Ibid., December 31, 1930, RG 59, DF 817.00 Johnson/171, NA.

[19] Capt. Alfred W. Johnson to Patrick J. Hurley, secretary of war, May 24, 1930, RG 59, DF 817.00 Johnson electoral mission/171, NA.

[20] Stimson to Johnson, June 13, 1930, RG 59, DF 817.00 Johnson electoral mission/20, NA.

activity. By late June, Sandino, who had returned from Mexico a month earlier, was attacking numerous United States-owned mines in the country's northeastern regions. Since the marine force had been reduced to less than 1,500 and its operation focused on training the National Guard, attempts to check the Sandino operation were generally ineffective. Johnson was also troubled to find President Moncada was taking unusual measures to insure a Liberal majority in areas where the Conservatives appeared well entrenched. For example, he found that large contingents of government-employed laborers in public works projects were moved in groups about the country for national security reasons. Yet, if these workers happened to be in a department for one month, they could register and vote there.[21]

Alarmed at the government's manipulation of a labor force, the captain thought he needed the same administrative authority McCoy had to ensure a free election. What Johnson did not realize was that Moncada and Díaz were different men both in temperament and as political leaders. The Liberal chief executive was a decisive, clever politician. Submission to Johnson's demands for closer election supervision meant subservience to the North American diplomat; Moncada would have none of that.

Johnson pressured the president to issue numerous decrees, among them freedom of the press and turning the country's entire communications network over to the national election board chairman. Moncada refused to comply with any of these requests. In total frustration, the election supervisor wrote Stimson, bitterly attacking the Nicaraguan chief executive. In one dispatch he said, "I cannot escape the conclusion that free exercise of political rights based on justice and common sense is in danger of being infringed." Johnson concluded with one of his many denunciations of the Nicaraguan leader by saying the president's absolute refusal to release those whom he considered unlawfully imprisoned Conservatives on his demand "would seriously prejudice the success of my mission."[22] What Johnson did, in effect, was to place the accomplishment of his assignment on Moncada's prompt fulfillment of all his requests for unlimited election supervision authority.

---

[21] Chamorro to Johnson, July 28, 1930, RG 43, Records, 1930 mission, entry 383, NA.

[22] Johnson to Stimson, August 13, 1930, RG 43, entry 371, NA.

Hanna opposed any ultimatum that would force Moncada to do anything which might weaken his position in the Liberal party. In fact, he saw no reason why the president was required to submit to any of Johnson's demands in the same manner Díaz had acquiesced to McCoy's requests. The North American diplomat justified his stand by noting that the political atmosphere in 1930 was not the same as it had been in 1928. Hanna was also well aware that a very proud and even stubborn politician now occupied the presidential chair. He was convinced any action that could injure his pride and force him to appear as a United States puppet might prove fatal to the entire supervision project. Furthermore, and of great significance, Hanna liked Moncada. The North American diplomat had made a special effort to cultivate the president's good will and friendship. He did not wish to see this close and cordial association wrecked by demands to issue a few amnesty decrees.[23] Even Stimson was disposed to give the president some benefit of the doubt in the feud with Johnson. The secretary merely hoped, as he said in one dispatch, "Moncada would act in good faith and comply with your [Johnson's] requests." Yet, Stimson had no intention of forcing him to do so.[24]

By the end of August 1930, Moncada still had not issued the decree providing Johnson with election supervision powers. As a result, the feud with Johnson intensified. Moncada insisted that compliance with all of the captain's demands would hurt him and diminish Liberal influence. The State Department finally lost its patience with the Nicaraguan leader and scoffed at his "prestige contention" by saying "this argument need not be given serious consideration."[25] Consequently, the United States directed the reluctant Hanna to warn Moncada of the serious consequences if he failed to cooperate, reasoning that if Moncada chose to ignore all the requests of the election supervisor in 1930, the more important 1932 elections might well be run by the Liberals without restrictions. The State Department's memo to Hanna on this subject reflected the United States' determination not to let this issue go unattended. It stated in part:

---

[23] Hanna to Johnson, August 11, 1930, RG 43, entry 371, NA.

[24] Johnson, personal log, July 1, 1930, RG 43, entry 346, NA.

[25] Memorandum, State Department, division of Latin American Affairs, August 15, 1930, RG 59, DF 817.00 Johnson/71, NA.

>You are authorized to remind President Moncada of
>the serious responsibility which this government
>has assumed by extending its cooperation to the
>government of Nicaragua in connection with its
>electoral problems, and that it is essential that the
>conditions under which this cooperation is carried
>out shall be such as to preclude the possibility of
>serious challenges in the future.[26]

Stimson reasoned that since Hanna had established good relations with the president, it was best to have him use his talents alone in prevailing upon Moncada to issue amnesty decrees and relinquish control over all communications operations during the election. Hanna succeeded in smoothing the ruffled feelings of the sensitive Moncada. On August 20, the president issued a decree that was considered at least symbolically important, releasing approximately fifty Conservatives from jail.

Johnson and the Conservatives vs. Moncada and the United States

Conservative leaders knew full well Johnson had a difficult task removing Liberals from key electoral positions and limiting the president's vast powers, but they did not abate their pressure. For example, both Díaz and Chamorro were opposed to the activities of the president's newly established "personal guard" — "volunteers" created to reinforce what Moncada thought to be the ineffective, marine-led National Guard. They were convinced, and correctly so, that the chief executive was using this military unit to nullify the National Guard's role as a police force in local communities. When this praetorian unit was first organized in January 1929, the marines, under the command of Moncada ally, General Logan Feland, thought it would reinforce the National Guard and allow the United States to withdraw troops from the war with Sandino more quickly. To the concern of many, it had become something of a "private army to do the personal bidding of the nation's chief executive.[27]

---

[26] State Department to Hanna, August 16, 1930, RG 59, DF 817.00 Johnson/72, NA

[27] Eberhardt to State Department, September 11, 1930, RG 59, DF 817.00/1051/258, NA. The marine commander, General Elias Beadle objected strongly to the "Volunteer Army." See Neill Macaulay, *Sandino*, 139.

The Conservative party wanted all of its elected municipal officers reinstated. They insisted that those who had been removed and replaced by Liberal party appointees in late 1929, during a state of siege when rebel raids had disrupted sections of the country, regain their posts. Under the constitution, the chief executive was empowered to remove local authorities during a "national crisis." Although Moncada rescinded the order proclaiming a state of siege in July 1930, he did not restore the legally elected Conservative municipal authorities in Chontales, Estelí, Jinotega, Nueva Segovia, or Matagalpa. Johnson correctly took note of the fact that these were regions where Conservatives enjoyed voting strength.

Captain Johnson sympathized with Díaz and Chamorro on this issue. He decided to make an all-out effort and compel Moncada to replace the legally elected Conservative officials in the municipalities where he had appointed Liberals. In fact, the captain was prepared to challenge the president openly in this matter. The implications in this were obviously significant and far-reaching. The United States supervisor was willing to battle the stubborn and proud Moncada over an election he was supervising without the Nicaraguan Congress's express approval.[28]

In early September 1930, Johnson confronted the issue and requested Moncada to remove his partisans from the 56 municipal governments and restore the duly elected Conservatives to their posts. "Your affirmative action in this case," Johnson said in writing to Moncada, "cannot fail to produce a most favorable reaction among all those who are interested in the success of free and fair elections."[29] The captain's suspicions about Moncada's intransigence were based on hard-core facts. On March 15, 1929, the Liberal government announced that the republic's regularly elected *alcaldes* (mayors) would not be returned to their positions until after the scheduled congressional elections in November 1930.[30] The Conservatives had something to worry about now. Johnson fully sympathized with their unfortunate position. If Nicaraguan politics remained true to form, a Liberal mayor in a predominantly Conservative area might not be entirely impartial when

---

[28] Johnson to State Department, September 11, 1930, RG 59, DF 817.00 Johnson/171, NA.

[29] Johnson to Moncada, September 12, 1930, RG 59, DF 817.00 Johnson/171, NA, Photocopy.

[30] *La Gaceta Oficial*, March 15, 1929.

officiating during an election.

However determined Moncada appeared to be in standing by his decision, Johnson tried to change the president's mind. Finally in a private meeting with the president on October 8, the captain and Hanna were able to persuade the chief executive to hold municipal elections in every department on the day of the congressional contests. When Johnson told the Conservatives this, they announced that their previous statement calling for voting abstention would be withdrawn.

Not less than a full day had passed when Moncada, in an about-face, informed Johnson that municipal elections would not be held after all. The president said the nominations for those offices had to be made 60 days before the election date. Obviously, if the letter of the law were to be respected, the president could keep his partisans in charge of the predominantly Conservative departments since election day was just one month away.[31]

The president's new position destroyed any rapport that still existed between Johnson and Moncada before this announcement. Bypassing regular diplomatic channels, the angry navy captain wrote Stimson a private note and said, "He [Moncada] had deceived both Mr. Hanna and myself." Johnson felt betrayed and related his thoughts on the matter to the State Department. The North American election supervisor had already promised the Conservatives that municipal elections would be held, and now it would be his unpleasant task to withdraw the pledge. He vividly and unequivocally revealed his feelings on the matter in a dispatch to the United States:

> ...this could be called a clever coup d'état. I believe that if the facts were generally known in the United States, public opinion would be scandalized. In view of the widely published reports in the United States heralding General Moncada's generous cooperation and desire for electoral freedom in Nicaragua, I believe that people of the United States are not acquainted with the facts. Moncada has violated the confidence of the United States. Every request that I have made of him which he has granted, he has granted in smaller measure than was granted to General McCoy in 1928. I believe the Department

---

[31]Johnson to Stimson, October 8, 1930, RG 59, DF 817.00 Johnson/ 97, NA.

should not allow the situation to go unchallenged.[32]

Surprisingly, the State Department did not interpret Moncada's action as being unreasonable at all. Stimson still had not lost confidence in the Liberal leader, even though at times he found him contentious and intractable. He was not about to criticize him for his stand on the municipal election issue. The secretary of state had no sympathy for Conservative efforts to secure removal of the Liberal-appointed *alcaldes.* He believed the Díaz/Chamorro demands were really part of a scheme to embarrass the Moncada government and put it on the defensive.[33]

Johnson threatened to resign his position unless Moncada relinquished some of his executive powers and permitted the North American to run the election alone. To prevent this embarrassing episode from happening and a Johnson/Moncada feud from erupting, the secretary of state decided to place Johnson directly under Hanna's direction in all matters dealing with presidential authority during the election.

Since Hanna and the chief executive had long since developed a close friendship, Stimson's solution was expected to solve the problem. The State Department did not see a need at this time for restricting the president's power as it had in 1928. According to the undersecretary of state, the United States was reasonably sure a fair election could be held, in his words, "without 100 percent victories over Moncada." Consequently, Johnson was relegated to a secondary position. Hanna was assigned to handle major problems involving election supervision with the president, a man both he and the U.S. government trusted.[34]

Hanna was not unmindful that the Conservatives were placed in a very difficult position. In five departments where they had the greatest numerical strength, appointed Liberal mayors would be in a position to exert undue influence on voters. He passed this rather unpleasant situation off merely as an "undesirable state of affairs." He pointed out that even though Moncada's partisans continued to occupy all the mayoral positions, Johnson could monitor the elections care-

---

[32] Ibid.

[33] Stimson to Johnson, September 11, 1930, RG 43, Records, 1930 mission, entry 371, NA.

[34] Undersecretary of State Joseph P. Cotton to Stimson, September 11, 1930, RG 59, DF 817.00 Johnson/269, NA.

fully. Hanna also suggested that since the United States did not plan to force Moncada to remove the appointed *alcaldes* by November, the 1931 municipal elections which followed might also be U.S.-supervised. The minister conceded that the Conservatives were justifiably worried with respect to the possible loss of all their power in a crucial period before the 1932 presidential election. Consequently, the legation pressed on and concluded a subsequent supervised municipal election in 1931. Hopefully, this would prevent Moncada from ousting all Conservative officeholders in districts where they had a majority of registered voters.[35]

Captain Johnson was forced to deliver the department's unpleasant decision regarding the 1930 municipal election question to the Conservatives. He considered it a particularly distasteful task. He was instructed to tell them the United States would not run local elections nor accept the Conservative demand for the removal of the Liberal-appointed *alcaldes*.

Johnson expressed his gratitude to the Conservatives for their faithful cooperation in all the preliminary election matters and informed them it was not his function to decide on the merits for the removal, appointment, or election of municipal officials. He concluded his message by saying it was his duty "to insure that the acts of such officials (*alcaldes*) shall not interfere with the free and fair election of Senators and Deputies this year (1930)."[36] The Conservatives predictably objected vehemently to Johnson's decision which they correctly concluded had been a direct order from Washington. As a reprisal, they warned that party members would not vote in the congressional elections. The United States was not concerned with the Conservative abstention tactic; at one point, the assistant secretary of state for Latin American affairs confidently remarked, "We can bury this [Conservative letter of protest] in the files." A rather limited but important objective had been achieved. President Moncada had not been further antagonized.[37]

---

[35] Hanna to State Department, October 2, 1930, RG 59, DF 817.00 Johnson/102, NA.

[36] Johnson to Roman Castillo, Conservative representative, national election board, November 1, 1930, Archivos del Tribunal Electoral Supremo, Managua.

[37] Assistant Secretary of State Francis White to Johnson, October 30, 1930, RG 59, DF 817.00/6895, NA.

An Election Victory Made to Order
and a Mission to 'Observe and Keep in Touch'

As Nicaragua's 1930 congressional elections approached, it was apparent President Moncada had relinquished few powers to U.S. election supervisors. It was also evident that the 13 U.S. election board chairmen and over 672 election personnel would not be able to persuade Liberal mayors and police officials to cooperate in registration proceedings. Also, without the assistance of local government officials, the election boards could not guarantee voters a safe trip to the polls for voting.[38]

Johnson admitted that Liberal mayors, not his staff, were actually running the congressional elections. In fact, he concluded that his subordinates had lost all control enforcing measures to guarantee citizens' safety on election day.[39] Since the U.S. Marine contingent had been reduced considerably, Johnson found he could not force his electoral program on Moncada. Even the National Guard had become a sort of governmental police force, and election board chairmen reported guardsmen were totally unreliable and not acting impartially.[40]

The U.S. electoral mission, with its supervisors including 200 marines and sailors, only partially supervised the 1930 congressional elections. Nine senators out of the 26-member upper house contested for seats. Twenty-two out of 43 of the deputies were to be elected to the Chamber of Deputies. Johnson, therefore, had a very big task with fewer assistants than General McCoy. With a smaller marine force, an admittedly ineffective National Guard, and Sandino's return from Mexico in spring of 1930, the U.S. election supervisors' prospects for insuring a free and fair election seemed remote.

Perhaps most disturbing of all — many seats were being contested in Nicaragua's predominantly Conservative departments. Unfortunately, these were areas where Moncada had retained his Liberal party appointees as mayors. The president

---

[38] Lloyd V.H. Durfee, chairman, election board, Department of Chontales, to Johnson, October 29, 1930, RG 43, Records, 1930 mission, folder 3-C-I, NA.

[39] Ibid.

[40] Chairmen, department election boards for Nueva Segovia, Estelí, Jinotega, and Chinendega, to Johnson, October 31, 1930, RG 43, Records, 1930 mission, entry 377, NA.

thought his control in these five Conservative regions was so important that he threatened to resign — raising the specter of subsequent political unrest — if the United States insisted that Liberal officeholders be removed.[41]

The chief executive knew the United States needed him at this time. The resignation threat proved effective. As Moncada had guessed, the State Department did not want to see a chaotic state of affairs emerge. Stimson relied on the Liberal leader to maintain domestic peace. The Liberals had a free hand to conduct elections in their own way. Johnson was relegated to the position of an observer.

In late September and early October, some 111,000 people registered to vote. On election day, November 8, only 60,000 people cast ballots. As expected, election results were decisive for the Liberals. Moncada's party won seven out of the nine contested Senate seats, and Liberals took 16 of the 22 races for deputy, reducing further Conservative membership in the Chamber of Deputies.

Election results were mixed. Carlos Cuadra Pasos was elected to the Senate from the predominantly Conservative department of Chontales. Yet Pedro Joaquín Chamorro, a leading journalist and a relative of Chamorro, lost his bid for an upper chamber seat in the overwhelmingly conservative area of Granada. The party leaders protested in vain even though votes cast in the election were 70 percent of those cast in 1928 in the same districts.

It was not difficult to conclude that Johnson had absolutely no authority in the election's administration. Moncada had successfully instructed his followers to carry out his orders, which they did of course. As a result, Congress was packed with Moncadistas.[42]

Reflecting on the results of the 1930 political contests, Captain Johnson belatedly asked his assistants for comments on the best course of action to take to prevent questionable elections in the future. Admiral C. H. Campbell, now commander of the U.S. Navy Special Service Squadron in Nicaragua, suggested that the United States immediately withdraw recognition from Moncada and establish a U.S. military government in the country, a proposal, incidentally that Sandino had

---

[41] Johnson, Memorandum, December 31, 1930, RG 59, DF 817.00 Johnson/171, NA.

[42] Ibid.

made in 1927. Needless to say, the State Department did not accept the squadron commander's view and even rejected the resignation plan. Consequently, the Liberal president retained U.S. good will and affection through 1930.[43]

When Captain Johnson returned home, he reported to Stimson that Moncada's retention of Liberal mayors in all the country's municipalities had paved the way for establishing a dominant Liberal organization, even a dictatorship. He believed this had created a decisive imbalance in the nation's political structure. He noted that the political situation gave the out party a perfect right to rebel against Moncada and either remove him forcibly from office or, in some way, insist on a liberalization of his policies. This proposition was in a sense urging the United States to change its pro-Liberal party position.[44]

Actually, Johnson was repeating and reemphasizing a suggested coup which Conservatives had made during the election. At that time, the U.S. legation had reported this promptly to Washington, in keeping with Hanna's sympathetic attitude toward the president. As could be expected, the captain's view of a coup d'état ending the Liberal regime was not accepted. In fact, Moncada had been able to retain a sizeable amount of good will and support both in the United States and among U.S. diplomatic personnel in Managua after the 1930 elections.

The Division of Latin American Affairs set forth the U.S. position with respect to future support of the Nicaraguan chief executive. In simple and plain terms, it justified the United States' unqualified backing of Moncada. In a memorandum advocating "no revolution," it noted and confirmed that Conservatives had remained in power until 1928 solely because of a United States military presence. The policy paper, therefore, concluded by referring to the political situation in 1930:

> United States Marines with full military equipment, including an aviation force, are stationed in the country, and marines control the Nicaraguan guard.

---

[43] Adm. C.H. Campbell, commander, Special Service Squadron, to Johnson, November 12, 1930, RG 43, Records, 1930 mission, entry 371, NA.

[44] Memorandum, Johnson to Stimson, December 30, 1930, RG 59, DF 817.00 Johnson/171, NA.

> In other words, it would now be futile, in the face
> of this North American military organization which
> is cooperating with the established Liberal govern-
> ment, for the Conservative party to undertake to
> obtain control of the government....[45]

Captain Johnson's suggestion that the United States support a Conservative coup was rejected outright. Yet, Washington had concluded that although the 1928 election was a free one, it had produced a dictator. Political stability in Nicaragua was still the United States' main objective in Central America, even while supervising elections.

Not long after Johnson had submitted his report, Secretary of State Stimson looked at the Nicaraguan question with more concern and interest. He knew President Hoover was apprehensive over the Nicaraguan problem as the U.S. Congress again was questioning the purpose for becoming involved there. Sandino also renewed his insurgent movement shortly after Johnson left Nicaragua in December 1930.

In March and April 1931, Sandino forces attacked areas on Nicaragua's east coast, and National Guard troops were ambushed there, killing eight marines. Moncada again wanted to reinforce his military position and add an auxiliary contingent to assist the National Guard. The U.S. minister agreed and allowed him to add 125 men to the guard forces. Actually, Moncada was dissatisfied with the unit's performance and expenses incurred. Renewed Sandino activity and Johnson's grim reports of Moncada's arbitrary actions in 1930, prompted a closer look at the Nicaraguan situation.

Sandino's continued military successes and Moncada's dictatorial actions focused attention on the chairmanship of the national election board, which was to be vacated again. If a Nicaraguan were appointed to succeed Johnson as the law prescribed, there was a chance Moncada might manipulate the upcoming 1931 municipal elections in such a way that subsequent U.S. supervision in 1932 would be impossible. Johnson, frustrated and exhausted, did not want to continue in the post. In fact, when he reached the United States in mid-December, he asked if it were possible for him to resign immediately.

---

[45] Memorandum on Major Price mission, State Department, division of Latin American Affairs, February 6, 1931, RG 59, DF 817.00 Johnson/207, NA. See also Stimson, Memorandum, February 5, 1931, RG 59, DF 817.00/1051/501, NA.

Stimson, not sure Moncada and his followers could be trusted to plan the important 1932 contest, wanted him to retain his position at least until a 1932 North American election supervisor could be selected. The United States decided it was not going to let time lapse in keeping a close watch over the Liberals between 1930 and 1932. Moreover, Moncada's conduct in the 1930 contests, as Johnson reported, had not enhanced the Central American's influence on the United States in the long run. As a precautionary measure, Stimson resorted to an interesting tactic for keeping a firm hand on election matters in Nicaragua through 1932.[46]

At this stage, Stimson was not ready to admit that Moncada had obstructed his project for creating political stability through election supervision leading to complete military withdrawal from the country. The secretary decided Johnson would keep his title as election board chairman even though a new assignment would take him away from Nicaragua. To keep in touch with developments in the republic, Stimson decided to have Major Charles F. B. Price, who had been working on election projects there since 1928, report on political developments during the 1931 municipal elections. He hoped that Price could be made at least vice-chairman of the election board and then try to conduct the duties of chairman. If this maneuver were accomplished, the major could restrain Moncada to some extent. The State Department wanted to use the earlier 1929 Nicaraguan request for election supervision, which had not stipulated specific contests, as a basis for Price's new assignment.[47]

The secretary of state made no public reference to his plan of having Price undertake this role. In fact, in February 1931, Stimson held a press conference and said an informal understanding at Tipitapa in 1927 had committed his government to supervise only the 1928 and 1932 presidential elections — no others. The secretary was firmly committed to a policy for withdrawing 1,000 of the 1,500 marines immediately, leaving the rest to be evacuated at the end of the 1932 elections. The specifics for maintaining control over elections were deliberately left out. The press corps was not advised that the U.S. government was to play an unofficial role in the 1931 municipal elections, thereby preparing to run the important presidential

---

[46] Stimson to Charles F. Adams, secretary of the U.S. Navy, January 21, 1931, RG 59, DF 817.00/6957, NA.

[47] Ibid., February 3, 1931, RG 59, DF 817.00 Johnson/175, NA.

election in 1932. The Price mission would, therefore, assist Stimson in reaching an important political objective as the military campaign against Sandino was a failure.

The State Department chose not to become too involved in the supervision of these local contests in 1931, even though Conservatives were hopeful Moncada's hand could be stayed this time. Price, therefore, was to perform a delicate task. He was directed to keep a close watch on all events and take note of the Liberal party's conduct and report his observations to the United States. Above all, he was to let the Nicaraguan officials know their activities were being watched.[48]

The United States soon learned that Moncada had his own plans for the national electoral board's operation in 1931. The wily Nicaraguan chief executive insisted that Price be allowed to take his post only if Washington planned to run municipal elections. The president correctly pointed out that no specific request had ever been made for a 1931 municipal election supervisor. As a result, Stimson decided not to force the issue. Enough adverse publicity had been given the controversial election business, and the secretary of state wanted no more. Anti-intervention sentiment in the United States Congress had some bearing on this decision, too. Consequently, he decided Price would hold no official position but could stay in Nicaragua only as an observer during the local election.[49]

Moncada's decision refusing to allow Price the chance to preside over the municipal elections concerned Stimson. Shortly after Price's observing functions had been clarified, the secretary directed the U.S. minister to obtain the president's quick assurances that the 1932 election would be supervised.[50] When carrying out this directive, Hanna found, to his regret, it was met with evasive replies and, at times, complete silence. Moncada's performance made Price's assignment even more important. As a result, his departure date for Nicaragua was moved up.

Price had learned about Nicaragua firsthand as a department election board chairman in 1928 and 1930. His task in 1931 was to gather information only, and he performed his job

---

[48] Memorandum on Major Charles Price mission, n.d. See also Stimson, memorandum, February 5, 1931, RG 59, DF 817.00/1051/501, NA.

[49] Stimson to Hanna, June 10, 1931, RG 59, 817.00 Johnson/211, NA.

[50] Ibid., June 15, 1931, RG 59, DF 817.00 Johnson/211, NA.

well. However, the United States was not sending a man to Nicaragua who was without prejudices or remained indifferent to the political controversy raging between Liberals and Conservatives. He was well aware Moncada had amassed a great deal of power — more, he thought, than should have been allowed during the 1930 elections.

As the chief executive had refused to honor Johnson's earlier requests for removing police powers from local Liberal mayors in 1930, Price was certain that Moncada would not relinquish his executive authority in 1932 either. Consequently, the North American observer strongly urged that a permanent U.S. election board chairman be appointed as soon as possible, even before the 1931 municipal elections. The major thought his accomplishments as an observer in the municipal elections would be negligible if an official U.S. election supervisor/fully powered chairman of the national election board were not present too.[51]

Since Price would be the only outside observer during the 1931 election, he decided to attend all the meetings of the national election board now headed by Nicaragua's vice-president, Enoc Aguado. Fortunately, a close friendship developed between the two men. As a result, the major was able to observe both the municipal elections and learn the nature of the Liberal party's internal feuds at close hand. Price saw the possibility of a Moncada/Aguado split within the Liberal party in 1931. Therefore, he cultivated his association with the vice-president, who was infinitely more cooperative than the president on election supervision matters.[52]

When Price began his work in the summer of 1931, he found the Conservatives unrealistically hopeful that they could win the municipal elections. They were certain his presence, at least, would pressure the Liberals to hold elections in all municipalities. However, the Conservatives' buoyed hopes did not impress the U.S. minister. Hanna believed the out party's optimism was excessive. His view was best revealed in a dispatch to the United States in July 1931. The report said the Conservatives failed to see the realities of the republic's political life and did not consider the importance of such factors as the "legitimate advantage which the Liberals will derive from

---

[51] Price to State Department, July 1, 1931, RG 59, DF 817.00 Johnson/268, NA.

[52] Price, report, n.d., RG 59, DF 817.00 Johnson/268, NA.

being in power."[53] Yet, Hanna was interested in a fair municipal election. In an adamant message to the vice-president, he noted that contests would have to be impartially supervised, as the United States had a great interest in these races prior to the 1932 election. In the same message, he implied that Washington's attitude toward the Liberals in 1932 would depend on the judicious manner in which they ran the election in 1931.[54]

Conservatives frequently urged Price to force Moncada to hold elections in each municipality since several departments went without elections in 1930. Liberal mayors appointed by the president still governed areas which were predominantly Conservative in voting strength. This was the case in at least five departments. Price prevailed upon Vice-President Aguado to have Moncada remove the appointees from the posts to which they had been appointed in 1929 and suggested to him if Moncada did so, it would be a master stroke of tact and diplomacy. The appeal to Moncada through the sympathetic, pliable vice-president failed. In early August, Conservatives held a convention and warned Moncada that if he did not remove his appointed municipal officers, the party would direct its followers to abstain altogether from casting votes in the upcoming elections.[55] Price interpreted this as a foolish ultimatum. He was sure the chief executive would not succumb to such pressure, particularly in the form of an open, direct challenge from his political opponents.[56]

Actually, the Conservative position in the matter was embarrassing to the United States. The refusal of one party to vote in the election cast a bad light on the Coolidge-Hoover administration's objective to reduce the bitter antagonism between the two groups and emphasize the democratic process. Moreover, plans to disengage from military intervention were already complicated by renewed Sandino raids in the northeast port of Cabo Gracido a Díos in March and April. At this point, the State Department also had decided not to protect North American citizens or property with troops, especially in the country's interior. By late spring, the guard, with limited United States Navy personnel and an aviation unit, had

---

[53] Hanna to State Department, July 17, 1931, RG 59, DF 817.00/7182, NA.

[54] Ibid., August 11, 1931, RG 59, DF 817.00 Johnson/244, NA.

[55] Managua *La Prensa*, September 2, 1931, 1.

[56] Op. cit.

effectively reduced rebel activity on the east coast, somewhat easing a direct Sandino threat to U.S. election plans from then on. Yet, the United States feared if one party claimed fraud or abstained from voting, people would surmise that the North American republic was failing in all its military and political objectives for establishing domestic peace.[57]

To prevent such an awkward situation from getting worse, the U.S. legation informed Chamorro and Carlos Cuadra Pasos that their ultimatum on the abstention plan would have to be withdrawn or at least modified in some significant way. Hanna was convinced their action had been particularly foolish since a threat not to vote merely ended any chance for negotiating the issue.[58]

After pressuring Chamorro and Cuadra Pasos to rescind their ultimatum, the U.S. legation convinced the Conservative leaders it was unwise to cancel elections in areas where municipal candidates wanted to run for office. The two conservative leaders promised that party members would be allowed to run but under the rather innocuous label of Independent Conservatives. Part of the wreckage had been salvaged in the form of a compromise. Price was then able to prevail upon Moncada to remove his appointees from municipal posts where elections had been held in 1927. While this did not replace all previously elected Conservative mayors, some were reinstated to their positions.

Price thought this was a fair solution as the president agreed to appoint Conservative mayors in these cities from a list of candidates drawn up by the out party. The ever-intractable Chamorro rejected the offer and insisted elections be held instead. The clever *caudillo* made a counter-proposal and, as oftentimes before, relying on his popular support, suggested that Congress decide the issue. On the surface, this seemed like an extraordinarily peculiar suggestion for a Conservative to make, inasmuch as the Congress was predominantly Liberal. However, Chamorro was certain that enough Liberals in the legislative body had become dissatisfied with Moncada's dictatorial rule that they would support the Conservatives on this issue and embarrass the president.[59]

---

[57] State Department to Hanna, April 16, 1931, RG 59, "Bandit activities, 1931/31," DF 817.00, NA.

[58] Hanna to State Department, September 12, 1931, RG 59, DF 817.00/7209. NA.

[59] Memorandum, Price, n.d., RG 59, DF 817.00 Johnson/245, NA. Interview with author, April 7, 1965.

When the Conservatives finally announced their abstention from all municipal elections, Price was convinced this
would do great damage to the party. He observed that people
would now consider the Conservatives "weak and cowardly."
More important, the major was sure the out party might
permanently lose a large measure of support from what he
called the "floating vote." He labeled these people the "band-
wagon boys who are always with the winning side." He was
convinced that any appeal to a segment of the electorate who
switched their allegiance from year to year would now be
permanently lost to the Liberals. He concluded that this would
place the Conservatives at a disadvantage in the critical 1932
presidential contest.[60]

Dissension in the Liberal Party Leadership

Major Price was displeased with the way Liberals supervised the various municipal contests. Likewise, he was not
confident elections could take place in all 13 departments as
the Sandino movement had successfully intensified its raiding
activities. After some persuasion, the North American observer
saw to it that some Independent Conservatives ran for office.
He was satisfied, at least, that a two-party contest would appear
to take place.[61]

In many cases, Price, even in his unofficial status, was
confronted with protests from both parties regarding registration and voting procedures. Yet more often than not, he
refrained from active involvement in local disputes. In some
matters, he actually made a decision for one side or the other
and relayed his findings to U.S. National Guard officers for
implementation. The marine commanders would then enforce
the decision on behalf of the "nonpartisan National Guard."[62]

Price's mission was not supposed to have succeeded or
failed as such. However, an assignment of this kind most
assuredly might have proved disastrous if it were undertaken
by a less able person. The marine major exerted his influence
unobtrusively and, for the most part, effectively. He never
earned Moncada's affection, nor did he expect to. Of greater
importance, he let the Nicaraguan leader know the United

---

[60] Price, report, n.d., RG 59, DF 817.00 Johnson/268, NA.

[61] Price to State Department, November 4, 1931, RG 59, DF 817.00
Johnson/254, NA.

[62] Ibid.

States was paying close attention to the country's internal political developments. Although Price did not undertake steps which directly challenged the president's authority, he concluded that if he had, chances for U.S. election supervision in 1932 might have been impeded or prevented altogether. Moreover, in 1931, continued Sandino activity, a major earthquake in Managua that nearly destroyed the city, and the very difficult management of the marine occupation itself raised serious questions as to the future course of a North American presence in Nicaragua. An era of retrenchment was about to begin.

The United States was now faced with the final test of its commitment to see that Nicaragua elected its principal leaders with election supervision. Moncada's Liberal followers, who were known as Gobiernistas, had long since consolidated their power. Now the stubborn, intractable chief executive posed a threat to United States policymakers. Stimson and even some U.S. Congressmen were unhappy with past military interventionist policies that had no political objectives. They wanted to withdraw the marines and see to it that both major parties contested fairly in the 1932 presidential election. This would outline what Stimson set out to do in 1928.

At one point during his assignment, Major Price referred to a possible split in the Liberal party and suggested its implications might be far-reaching and helpful to the United States. Hanna also had become aware of Moncada's political troubles. In late autumn of 1931, in a dramatic step, the politically ambitious vice-president met with the North American diplomat. Aguado had developed a close personal relationship with Hanna, too — far better than most of the Liberal leaders among the Gobiernistas. He wasted no time in explaining the purpose of his visit. In a bitter denunciation, he told Hanna the Liberal party was about to split and that Moncada had been using the party for his personal gain. He said the president had refused to allow a considerable segment of the party membership, particularly from León, to participate in his administration. Moreover, he pointed out, Moncada had never allowed elections for membership on the party's national governing board either. He was convinced that this executive arm of the party would dominate the Liberals' upcoming national convention and place a Moncada puppet in the presidency for another four years.

The vice-president, therefore, proceeded to unveil a maneuver to stop this so that a new movement in the party would be formed called the Liberal Conciliation and Reorganization Faction. Its governing body, the central board, would conduct all the group's activities. If Moncada then refused to allow new elections for the party's regular governing board, Aguado assured Hanna his followers would nominate its own candidate for president, even a U.S.-approved candidate, he said. The vice-president received no assurances for support at this time but did later.

Hanna immediately reported this significant and important development. He also confirmed Aguado's complaint that Moncada had ignored party procedure in not holding regular elections to the party's executive board. In fact, Hanna was maneuvering the Aguado faction within the Liberal party.[63]

When Hanna called on the president, Moncada conveyed his thoughts on Nicaragua's political future to a man he trusted. Undoubtedly, the president believed he was talking to a confidant. The Nicaraguan chief executive pointedly recalled that in 1928 he had hoped to establish a constitutional regime based on the objectives laid down at the 1927 Tipitapa conference. He also noted that the Díaz government had to resort to unconstitutional acts, such as issuing executive decrees in 1928 to implement the election law agreement made with Stimson. As a result, he said the chief executive then had to ignore congressional prerogatives on numerous matters, even the decree establishing the National Guard, to insure that election procedures were established.

Pressing further, in his conversation with Hanna, the president mentioned that the supervision of the 1928 and 1930 elections was undertaken by executive decrees, ignoring the legislature's prerogative to canvass and issue the election results. In fact, as he pointed out, his own election in 1928 was, in a strict, legal sense, illegal. The law prescribed Congress's certification of the 1928 election. Yet, it was the United States-run national election board, not Congress, that had certified the election. Moncada told Hanna he wanted to amend the constitution, making all the foregoing acts retroactively legal. He dropped his political bombshell and suggested that the president's term be extended from four to six years. He proposed canceling the 1932 elections and suggested instead that Congress elect a provisional president in January 1933 to serve for one year. After the constitution was amended,

---

[63] Hanna to State Department, November 3, 1931, RG 59, DF 817.00/7241, NA.

Congress would elect a president for the six-year term beginning in 1934.

The astute Hanna saw what Moncada really had in mind. He pointed out in a later dispatch to Stimson that Moncada told him "an extension of his [Moncada's] term might be forced upon him." In any case, the North American diplomat made a quick counter-proposal to check Moncada's project. He suggested that presidential elections be held as scheduled in 1932, with the stipulation the person elected would serve four years if a constitutional amendment providing for a six-year term failed to pass. The minister also insisted elections be held in 1932 even if a six-year term were accepted. The president-elect in 1936 would then begin the adopted six-year term. Hanna was holding fast to the United States election supervision plan for 1932.[64]

Moncada said his plan was better and would pursue it anyway. Although disturbed with the chief executive's new strategy, the State Department's Legal Affairs Division concluded that the Liberal leader's proposal, although devious, was based on sound, legal grounds. Moncada's project was a clever one as the constitution prohibited a president from succeeding himself. However, if Congress elected a provisional chief executive other than the incumbent in 1933, Moncada would be eligible for election to a six-year term if a constitutional amendment were adopted in 1934.[65] Vice-President Enoc Aguado's earlier warning to the U.S. legation of Moncada's plans for rejecting a 1932 election was substantiated.

When Juan Bautista Sacasa, now the Nicaraguan minister to the United States, observed that the constitution needed amending with respect to the election law, the United States became genuinely uneasy. Sacasa was convinced that the time had come for Congress to legalize the 1928 and 1930 executive decrees which prohibited his countrymen from heading election boards. The flagrant disregard of the constitution bothered the sensitive and fair-minded Sacasa. Still, Stimson wasted little time rejecting proposals for changing it, as Moncada's party held a sizeable margin in Congress. Sacasa then offered a compromise suggesting elections be postponed for two years and a military commander head the government. Stimson turned this suggestion aside. Sacasa then dropped further

---

[64] Ibid., October 8, 1931, RG 59, DF 817.00/7270, NA.
[65] Ibid.

mediation efforts and agreed to abide by the 1932 election supervision.[66] He had good reason to be cooperative since his well-known presidential aspirations would improve as the Moncada government became less and less popular.[67]

In time, the Aguado faction felt confident that Moncada had made himself totally unacceptable to the United States with his designs for continuing in office beyond his four-year term. Therefore, the Leónese group, headed by the vice-president, decided to support unqualifiedly the 1932 election supervision project and ask the North American legation to select a candidate for them. The minister diplomatically refused but did nothing to discourage the group's pro-U.S. activities, either. Essentially, the president had become uncooperative, even potentially disruptive, in the election supervision project. The León Liberals now offered the United States a chance to implement two major foreign policy objectives in Nicaragua: the retention of a North American-run national election board to insure the 1932 presidential election and, at the same time, final arrangements for withdrawing all military personnel by the end of 1932.[68]

---

[66] Memorandum of conversation of Stimson and Sacasa, December 31, 1931, RG 59, DF 817.00/7286, NA.

[67] Sacasa to State Department, December 23, 1931, RG 59, DF 817.00/7266, NA.

[68] Hanna to State Department, December 4, 1931, RG 59, DF 817.00/7266, NA.

Photo courtesy of the Still Pictures Branch, United States National Archives

MANAGUA, NICARAGUA. The U.S. Marine Band marches on inauguration day, January 1, 1933.

VIII

Politics Make Strange Bedfellows: 1932

The Dispatch of an Election Supervisor

DURING THE MUNICIPAL ELECTIONS in 1931, the United States anticipated sending another election supervisor to prepare for the 1932 contest. Numerous officials, both in the United States and Managua, were convinced Moncada was preparing to postpone or cancel the election altogether. Certainly, the president's feelings about a constitutional amendment for the 1932 contest made the issue of prime interest and concern. The United States concluded that if a new chairman was dispatched soon, Moncada's political maneuverings might end or at least be curtailed.

Secretary of State Stimson, therefore, set about to find a candidate. The navy department suggested Rear Admiral Clark Howell Woodward, who had been an aide to General McCoy in his mission to China in 1905. Stimson, who knew him well, responded favorably to the choice and recalled how greatly impressed he was with him during the 1927 Nicaraguan peace negotiations. At the time, Woodward was the commanding officer of the *USS Milwaukee*, located off the west coast of the republic. He had commanded 1,800 sailors who were sent ashore that year to establish peace in the area.[1]

Woodward had some previous experience dealing with Latin American political figures. A veteran of the Spanish American War and with service experience in the Philippines, he served in Brazil and Peru in the early 1920s as head of the United States naval mission in both countries. In 1923, he became chief of the Peruvian naval general staff and served in this post until 1926. From 1928 to 1931, he was acting governor

---

[1] Memorandum, State Department, division of Latin American affairs, December 5, 1931, RG 59, DF 817.00/7275, NA.

of the Canal Zone in Panama. Many U.S. officials considered him the most qualified officer on active service who could handle the delicate and sensitive Nicaraguan assignment. Stimson took him to see President Hoover who wanted to meet him and be assured personally that an end to the military involvement in Nicaragua could be achieved.[2]

While preparations were made to send Woodward to Central America, Willard Beaulac, the United States chargé d'affaires in Nicaragua, reported that Vice-President Enoc Aguado had agreed to resign his post as chairman of the national election board as soon as Woodward arrived. Aguado was anxious to demonstrate his support for a supervised election, which would improve his chances for ending Moncada's political dominance and enhancing his own.

Beaulac wanted Woodward sent down quickly as well because Moncada had made known his plan to fill the chairmanships of all election boards in late 1931. According to the 1923 Dodds' law then in effect, this was supposed to be done by January 1 during an election year.[3] The Department of State directed Beaulac to watch all of Moncada's activities, especially with regard to legislation reforming the Dodds law. The United States had every intention of using a 1930 law instead, which gave the election supervisor considerable power to run the presidential contest.[4]

To forestall a Moncada coup thwarting the 1930 law, Woodward flew to Managua on January 4, 1932, for a "familiarization visit." His early arrival convinced Moncada that his plan for extending the presidential term was no longer to be tolerated.[5]

Stimson was resolved not to allow the ambitious Nicaraguan president another four years as chief executive. Outwardly, however, the secretary wisely maintained a friendly attitude toward him. He made it perfectly clear privately to the Nicaraguan leader that he would not retain his office beyond the duly constituted four years. Stimson disclosed his decision

---

[2] Stimson, Diary, entry January 1, 1932.

[3] Beaulac to State Department, December 12, 1931, RG 59, DF 817.00/7279, NA.

[4] State Department to U.S. legation, Managua, December 22, 1931, RG 59, DF 811.00/727a, NA.

[5] U.S. legation, Managua, to State Department, January 16, 1932, RG 59, DF 817.00 Woodward electoral mission/31, NA.

to the president in the best of diplomatic language. The secretary responded to a letter which Moncada had written suggesting some form of constitutional reform that extended his power. Fortuitously, the Nicaraguan president did not mention his proposal to lengthen term of office. Stimson seized this intentional or unintentional omission in the following note to him:

> I should be wanting in frankness if I failed to say to you that I rejoice to find no mention of this proposal [having Congress elect a provisional president for one year]...and that I am, therefore, able to conclude that you have found it advisable to abandon this project....You must realize that your sincerity would be questioned by many if you attempted to carry out the plan...and that it would undoubtedly contribute to suspicion and factional feeling. Moreover, I see serious obstacles to such an arrangement insofar as concerns the assistance to be given by my government in connection with the next presidential elections in Nicaragua. The government of the United States is confident that your government will take whatever steps are appropriate and necessary in order that the electoral mission may have the full authority required to carry out its task.[6]

The secretary of state concluded his letter by adding these prophetic words that surely were not difficult for the Nicaraguan president to understand: "I congratulate you on this [the way Moncada had handled himself in the past] and have every confidence that you will round out your administration in such a way as to merit unstinted praise."[7] Clark Howell Woodward's early visit to Nicaragua, on Stimson's advice, lent force and credence to the warning. The note must have been effective. Moncada never mentioned reforming the constitution again.

There was nothing extraordinary or unusual in a Nicaraguan presidential aspirant visiting the United States to seek an endorsement for his candidacy. The 1932 election year was no exception to this practice. In late autumn 1931, the *Excelsior,* a newspaper in the eastern department of Bluefields, reported

---

[6] Letter, Stimson to Moncada, December 9, 1931, RG 59, DF 817.00/7271, NA, Photocopy.

[7] Ibid.

that its senator, Rodolfo Espinosa, at one time foreign minister in Juan Bautista Sacasa's Constitutionalist government on the east coast (and later elected vice-president in 1932), made a trip to the United States. His hometown paper speculated that he was actually looking for U.S. support for the Liberal party's presidential nomination. The *Excelsior* was correct. Espinosa did make the pilgrimage to Washington to see Stimson and sound out the secretary's feelings regarding his candidacy.

It did not take the legislator long to learn the State Department's reaction to his presidential ambitions. As the conversation with Stimson turned to the subject of Sacasa, the Secretary of State pointedly remarked that as the Nicaraguan Minister he was one of "my very best friends" in the United States. At this time, the former vice-president's name had been prominently mentioned as a possible presidential candidate, and people were aware the Hoover administration had not expressed any displeasure toward it. When Espinosa heard Stimson's declaration of friendship for Sacasa, he, an experienced politician familiar with U.S. influence in his country's politics, promptly returned home and canceled his own campaign for the presidency.[8]

In early 1932, Vice-President Enoc Aguado began organizing his faction's opposition to President Moncada. Liberal party members from León were certain their support was considerably stronger than the president's. Woodward recalled in his January trip to Nicaragua that he also was convinced Moncada did not command the widespread backing he claimed. In fact, the admiral, not incorrectly, believed the chief executive actually imposed his candidacy on the Liberal party in 1928 by virtue of his association with Stimson at Tipitapa. Therefore, the 1930 U.S. election board chairman considered him not a bona fide Liberal but merely an opportunist. Aguado was fully aware of this view.[9]

In any case, Sacasa was confident his bid for the presidency would not be discouraged in the United States. Unashamedly, he told the State Department in January 1932 that he believed he would be forced to accept the nomination of the Liberal party. As vice-president, he considered himself the legitimate successor to President Solórzano, who was

---

[8] Stimson, Diary, entry October 30, 1931.

[9] Adm. Clark Howell Woodward, report, June 1932, RG 59, DF 817.00/231, NA.

ousted in 1926. Although Stimson made no statement endors-
ing him, he recorded in his diary when bidding farewell to the
Nicaraguan diplomat that he "gave the minister all kinds of
advice on the best way to develop the country economically
and stop banditry." He also offered the Nicaraguan emissary
some unsolicited advice on how to govern a "politically
unstable people."[10]

Candidates for the Liberal party nomination then appealed to their counterparts in other Central American states.
The Liberal Guatemalan President Jorgé Ubico (1931-1944),
who was particularly anxious to extend his influence throughout the area, received pleas from Leonardo Argüello, Rodolfo
Espinosa, Vice-President Enoc Aguado, Juan Bautista Sacasa,
and even José Moncada for assistance in their quest for the
party's nomination.[11] The Guatemalan liked Sacasa least of all.
For him, the latter had close ties with Mexico's President
Plutarco Elias Calles. Earlier, the Nicaraguan had signed a pact
with Ubico's northern neighbor whereby Mexico would provide military assistance to Sacasa's campaign opposing the
U.S.-backed Díaz regime in 1927.[12]

Although Ubico backed Aguado and Espinosa for president and vice-president respectively, the Guatemalan *caudillo*
ultimately accepted Sacasa as the party's choice. He concluded
that it was more in Guatemala's interest to have a Liberal than
a Conservative as Nicaragua's chief executive.[13]

Moncada's plans for amending the constitution and
establishing a provisional government still posed a serious
problem for the United States. Even though Woodward had
made his survey trip in early January, he was not to stay long.
His observations were by no means encouraging since he was
convinced Moncada was still preparing a scheme to avoid the
1932 election. President Hoover's announcement that all
remaining marines would be withdrawn in 1932 may have
given the president encouragement to proceed with plans to
continue in office beyond his regular term. The national
election board's North American vice-chairman proposed, as a

---

[10] Stimson, Diary, entry January 11, 1932.

[11] Kenneth Grieb, *Guatemalan Caudillo: The Regime of Jorgé Ubico, Guatemala 1931-1934* (Athens: University of Ohio Press, 1979), 102.

[12] Ibid.

[13] Ibid., 103-104.

precautionary measure, a contingency plan whereby some two thousand marines would be sent to the republic to prepare for the election. If the Nicaraguan chief executive were about to defeat or ignore the León Liberals, then election board officials had to contemplate some kind of force to impress upon him U.S. determination to run the 1932 presidential election.

The proposed marine offshore, "show of force" operation was to be implemented in two parts. One force would leave Quantico, Virginia, on July 6, 1932, and be deployed on Nicaragua's east coast. Troops assigned to security guard duty in the country's western part would leave sometime before July 20, assisted by Special Service Squadron elements located on ships off both Nicaraguan coasts.[14]

At this point, Stimson quickly stepped in to end the "show of force" plan. He was convinced the Sandino problem had to be solved by Nicaraguans alone. Therefore, the large-scale marine occupation plan was summarily rejected. The secretary of state insisted that marines no longer be engaged in direct combat with rebel forces. Instead, he wanted a limited number of U.S. troops concerned with election supervision only.[15] In fact, the secretary of state had been disappointed with marine operations in Nicaragua for a long time and, at this point, was certain they were not equipped to handle guerrilla warfare tactics. In spring of 1931, when Sandino was raiding U.S. mines and lumber businesses in the Puerto Cabézas area, the secretary of state resolved to withdraw the marines from the conflict. They seemed inept in defeating the Nicaraguan rebel militarily or even isolating his activities. Therefore, plans proposed by United States election supervisors to enlarge the marine contingent substantially were not adopted — nor, for that matter, was Congress willing to increase funds later for election supervision.[16]

Although the 1932 presidential race was to be the last supervised election, Stimson was determined Moncada would not obstruct voting procedures as he had done in 1930 and 1931. The State Department resolved to make the 1932 contest successful even if it meant preventing Moncada from exercis-

---

[14] Price to Chief Naval Officer, February 17, 1932, RG 59, DF 817.00 Woodward electoral mission/30, NA.

[15] Stimson, Diary, entry May 9, 1932.

[16] Stimson to U.S. Minister, Nicaragua, April 16, 1931, *Foreign Relations* 2: 808.

ing any influence in the Liberal party and allowing marines to operate election boards directly. Yet, he was concerned that if marines conducted registration and voting in rebel-held areas, they might come into military contact with Sandino.[17]

At this time, the United States did not want the final stage in Stimson's 1927 plan: an electoral law introduced for passage in the Nicaraguan Congress that provided for a U.S. election board chairman and 13 departmental presidents. The decision was passed on political reality. In early 1932, the legation studied the congressional membership and found that Moncada had enough votes to defeat a measure of this kind.

During the spring, President Moncada announced that his government could no longer afford to finance the National Guard or pay the U.S. electoral mission expenses. This decision posed a formidable threat as most of the guard commands were held by Nicaraguans. Stimson readily admitted he was faced with a grave challenge and knew he could not obtain money from the United States Congress, which in June refused to appropriate more money to send 500 marines to Nicaragua. It seemed to him incongruous, on the one hand, to tell the legislative branch that U.S. Marines were being withdrawn from Nicaragua and, at the same time, request sums to finance another kind of intervention project.[18]

The secretary of state directed the United States legation in Managua to present a choice to the president, and it was a risky proposal at best. It said, "Provide [$] 25,000 a month for June, July, August, and September for the election supervision, or the Hoover government would immediately withdraw the marines and cancel the election supervision."[19] Hanna promptly began his diplomatic gamble. On May 5, he turned to Anastasio Somoza Garcia, a close associate of Moncada who had served as deputy minister for foreign relations, efficiently handling the

---

[17] Memorandum, State Department, March 25, 1932, RG 59, DF 817.00 Woodward electoral mission/44-1/2, NA. Woodward wanted 1,800 more marines for the election. The State Department rejected this but finally decided to send 645 electoral personnel to "peaceful regions" but no protective military force. See Kamman, *Search for Stability*, 212.

[18] Stimson, Diary, entry April 5, 1932. Both Senators William Borah and Robert Lafollette had applauded Stimson's withdrawal plan.

[19] Stimson to U.S. legation, Managua, May 24, 1932, RG 59, DF 817.00 Woodward electoral mission/70, NA.

troubles accompanying the 1931 earthquake. He became chief designate of the National Guard. Hanna explained the possibility for withdrawing the marines if the money were not forthcoming. Somoza, in his flawless English, aware of the primacy of security interests for the United States, responded by warning that the costs of a marine departure would likely precipitate the fall of Moncada's government, creating the prospect of a Sandino victory. Somoza was convinced that the president's diminishing popularity was doing considerable harm to the party and without a large military establishment, the Liberals could possibly be ousted from power.

Hanna agreed with the deputy foreign minister's observations. Yet, Somoza delivered the message to Moncada anyway. On May 26, the Nicaraguan president announced that $25,000 a month would be placed at Woodward's disposal from the government's budget. Hanna reported to Stimson that "Somoza's 10 minutes with the president helped me."[20]

A Liberal Power Struggle

When Vice-President Enoc Aguado presented his plan to Hanna for creating a new faction in the Liberal party, his strategy apparently was not taken very seriously. It seemed Moncada had created a formidable political machine. There was little indication that he could be removed from office or dislodged from his party's leadership. However, by spring of 1932, the Leónese Liberals, or the Triangulos, as they were now called, consisting of Aguado, Sacasa, and Espinosa, gathered a considerable amount of the party's popular support. They no longer appeared to be a minor dissident faction. It was evident they had to be given more attention. Obviously, they could be useful to Washington's strategy for successfully completing an election supervision project.

The Triangulos' principal objective was to remove Moncada from power within the party. They concluded his dictatorial rule since 1928 had alienated most elements in the Liberal organization — the most offensive violation being Moncada's repeated unwillingness to hold required elections for the Liberal party's national governing board every two years. Moncadistas who were appointed to the governing body in 1927 had never stood for election. Actually, many Liberals who

---

[20] Hanna to Stimson, May 27, 1932, RG 59, DF 817.00 Woodward/ 87, NA.

followed the Triangulos had been close associates of Sacasa in his provisional government at Puerto Cabézas in 1927. Since Moncada had made his peace with the Conservatives through Stimson at Tipitapa, Sacasistas did not look upon his action favorably. Some, in fact, considered it treason. In any case, the origins of this crucial split had begun before the 1928 elections.

Moncada had his own candidate for president now that he had decided not to revise the constitution. He chose Minister of Finance Antonio Barbarena. Even though Barbarena was considered to have had Moncada's official blessing, the lega-tion was not convinced that the president had lost hope for remaining in office.

In November 1931, for the first time since 1927, Liberals held a national convention and rejected Moncada's request to leave the governing board intact. In a convention floor vote, the powers of the governing body were drastically reduced in a significant test of strength of both factions. Moncada emerged from the struggle in a noticeably weaker position. In fact, the governing board was subjected to general party convention dictates. Moncada continued to ignore the change in party rules and decided to call his own conclave in February 1932. During the earlier November 1931 meeting, a commission of electoral control was selected by vote of the assembled delegates. That body was directed to supervise the selection of representatives to the nominating convention for president in 1932. Conse-quently, Moncada was to recognize only the party's governing board as its true executive arm. The Triangulos from León accepted only the party convention decisions, and the commis-sion of electoral control decided to postpone challenging Moncada. They very wisely waited until Woodward returned in June, expecting him to settle the matter in their favor then.

It was not difficult to see Moncada had played a singularly dictatorial part in this dispute. Since he prevented the national convention delegates from adopting rules for the nominating procedure, he also did not want to risk losing control of the popular convention. These tactics consequently tarnished his image. Even though the president was in control of many local party organizations, he was faced with a majority of delegates who opposed his arbitrary tactics.[21]

As could be expected, the State Department pondered

---

[21] León *El Comercio,* June 18, 1932, 1, and *La Nación* June 17 and 21, 1932, 1 (both Liberal newspapers).

how to solve the feud. A settlement had been reached in 1928 under similar circumstances in the Conservative party. Yet this was a particularly difficult problem in 1932 because a shrewd, stubborn, and uncooperative president was involved, not a pliable chief executive like Adolfo Díaz.

Some officials in the State Department suggested that the Nicaraguan Supreme Court examine the matter and decide which faction was the bona fide group, the national governing board or the general party convention. Many in the United States recalled the same problem had occurred when General Enoch Crowder was sent to Cuba (1919-21) to revise electoral laws. At that time, the Supreme Court had made a decision satisfactory to all groups in the matter. But the proponents of this solution for Nicaragua's difficulties were reminded promptly that Moncada had appointed all the incumbent Supreme Court justices.[22]

The Gobiernistas, or Moncada faction, refused to participate in the February nominating convention, which was called by the delegates at the November 1931 conclave. The Leónese group planned to wait until Woodward arrived in June. Aguado, Sacasa, and Espinosa were certain that their forces were now strong enough to defeat the president.

When Woodward reached Managua, he started to work on the administrative details of election supervision and, of course, faced the Liberal party's internal crisis. Vice-President Aguado resigned his post as planned and began a campaign to defeat the Gobiernistas. He was sure that if he vacated his position, Woodward would tackle the Liberal dispute sooner and more effectively.

The issues surrounding the controversy between the Gobiernistas and Triangulos were not complicated. The former claimed that the party statutes recognized the national governing board as the executive body, and only its decisions were binding, not those of an assembled convention of delegates. The Triangulos insisted this organization did not reflect the feelings of party regulars; therefore, its membership had to be changed.[23] The national election board chairman had formed his opinion (favoring the Triangulos) and did not waver as to

---

[22] Memorandum, State Department, May 12, 1932, RG 59, DF 817.00/7410, NA.

[23] National Election Board, Sessions 34, 35, 36, and 37, June 1932, RG 43, Records, 1932 mission, entry 387, NA.

which side commanded the greatest support in the party.[24] Woodward was, however, a wise and astute diplomat and initially remained noncommittal. He was convinced that if he made a premature decision while both sides were arguing their cases, it might aggravate the situation.

Many Liberal newspapers suggested a plebiscite be held electing delegates to a national convention. Those who urged the plebiscite thought that if one took place Juan Bautista Sacasa would win easily.[25] The North American election board chairman agreed since he was certain a popular vote would relieve him of having to pick one group. He was also convinced Moncada might not win in a popular election of this kind with the Leónese faction. Woodward thought a Sacasa victory would end the president's hold on the party and permanently remove him as a political force in the Liberal camp.[26] The admiral finally made his move and decided the commission of electoral control, previously appointed by the 1931 Liberal party convention, would conduct the plebiscite. Woodward's decision pleased Sacasa's group because Triangulos dominated the committee.

Woodward was confident his decision to hold a plebiscite was both a popular and important one. The U.S. election staff and the legation felt Sacasa was the most popular figure in the party. The decision to support a plebiscite proposal was actually designed to help one faction and one person: the Triangulos and Sacasa. Now a popular anti-Moncadista would be assisted immeasurably towards a presidential nomination in which the party's rank and file could express its preference.[27] As could be expected, President Moncada was incensed at the admiral's decision. He accused him of not being impartial at all, which was true. When the electoral commission was selected to run the plebiscite, its members were all identified as Leónese Liberals.

The president knew his governing board had suffered a major defeat and said party statutes required only the supreme

---

[24] U.S. electoral mission, intelligence section, Diary, July 12, 1932, RG 43, Records, 1932 mission, entry 387, NA.

[25] *El Comercio*, June 22, 1932, 1.

[26] Woodward, memorandum, July 7, 1932, RG 59, DF 811.00 Woodward/231, NA.

[27] U.S. legation, Managua, intelligence report, July 7, 1932, RG 59, DF 817.00 Woodward/7483, NA.

governing board to run all plebiscites and primaries. The chief executive's view actually rested on a firm legal basis, whereas Woodward's decision was a direct assault on Moncada's political organization. Even Hanna admitted that Moncada's point was well taken and Woodward's decision not an impartial one. Justifiably, the legation was somewhat alarmed when Moncada advised the minister that Nicaragua would never accept the Woodward decision.[28]

Whatever might have been the significance of Moncada's remark, the Gobiernistas and Triangulos prepared to contest for delegate posts anyway. During the period preceding the plebiscite, Moncada, for the first time, became less accessible to the legation and Woodward's staff. In fact, North Americans in Managua were convinced and relieved that Moncada's expected defeat in the plebiscite really meant a victory for Sacasa, a candidate who now supported a U.S.-supervised election.[29]

Woodward had refused to recognize the Gobiernistas' and Triangulos' governing bodies. Yet, he permitted a general party convention composed of Triangulo sympathizers to appoint a committee and to run a plebiscite under the watchful, sympathetic eyes of the legation and election board staff.[30]

The election board chairman designed a further strategy which was ultimately to seal Moncada's fate in his war with Sacasa. The yankee captain's colleagues were to praise his maneuver in this endeavor highly. In fact, some veteran diplomats in Managua called it one of the most clever political tactics ever made by a North American in the country.[31] Just before the plebiscite took place, Woodward obtained a promise from Sacasa, Aguado, and Espinosa that the candidate receiving the most delegate support at the convention would in turn be backed by all others. This, said Woodward, was a "pact of honor." At first, Leonardo Argüello, Moncada's former

---

[28] Hanna to State Department, July 22, 1932, RG 59, DF 817.00 Woodward/131, NA.

[29] Major Charles Price, report, July 9, 1932, RG 59, DF 817.00 Woodward/120, NA.

[30] Woodward to Junta Directiva Nacional y Legal Liberal (León and Managua), July 18, 1921, Archivos del Tribunal Electoral Supremo, Managua.

[31] U.S. legation, Managua to State Department, August 1, 1932, RG 59, DF 817.00 Woodward/183, NA.

foreign minister and now his choice for president, could hardly resist the chance to place his "honor" before the Liberal voters. The Moncada faction knew full well they might suffer a defeat if they did not pledge themselves to conduct a fair campaign for delegates. Both sides were keenly sensitive of public opinion and fought desperately to keep their activities honest.[32]

Just before the plebiscite took place on July 20, Argüello, who fully realized he had committed himself to accept a Triangulo victory if he lost, urged his followers not to vote nor to follow Woodward's direction in his "pact of honor." Argüello insisted later that this action was merely a device to secure a Sacasa victory and nothing more.[33] Then, obviously after some reflection, Moncada's candidate went ahead anyway and signed the "pact of honor." As a result, on balloting day, the Argüello backers were widely split; some followed his earlier announcement and refused to vote. Others, remembering he had signed the agreement, participated in the primary. The Gobiernistas paid a heavy price for this blunder, as well over 50 percent of the delegates selected in the plebiscite were pledged to vote for Sacasa. Woodward was elated and correctly surmised that "this ended Moncada's tyrannical dictatorship over the party.[34]

Woodward cleverly had maneuvered the Gobiernistas into signing a pledge with the Triangulos. Obviously, the Moncada followers did so half-heartedly as they knew a Leónese-run plebiscite meant defeat. Yet, how could Argüello refuse to be "honorable"? He sealed his fate when he told his followers to reject the pact and then went ahead and signed it.

On July 26, Liberals nominated Sacasa, the Harvard-trained, medical-doctor-turned-diplomat, as their presidential candidate and Adolfo Espinosa, the senator from Bluefields, as his running mate. At long last, the former vice-president was nearing the presidency he had been denied by the United States in 1927. Now, the North American government did everything possible short of direct, open support to place him in office.[35]

[32] Managua *La Prensa*, August 9, 1932, *La Nacion*, August 10, 1932, and *Diario Moderno*, August 14, 1932, 1.

[33] Managua *Diario Moderno*, July 19, 1932, 1.

[34] Woodward, report, RG 59, DF 817.00 Woodward/231, NA.

[35] Woodward to Stimson, August 1, 1932, RG 43, Records, 1932 mission, entry 384, NA.

Politics — The Art of the Possible

Since 1928, the Conservatives had experienced the disadvantage of being out of power. Both the 1930 and 1931 elections had by no means offered them any real chance to reduce Liberal domination in the republic. Now, in 1932, a North American had undertaken again the responsibility for supervising an election. This time Conservatives were hopeful they could defeat a Liberal. No one doubted, least of all the Conservatives, that Sacasa would make a formidable opponent — far more effective, in fact, than Leonardo Argüello, the somewhat colorless former foreign minister. In any case, the Conservatives drew up a list of election safeguards which they hoped Woodward would carry out as they were exactly the same ones the Liberals made in 1928.

The Conservative party's governing board asked for a number of actions, among them full amnesty decrees, local police, removal of revenue guards, and telegraph and telephone lines placed under strict U.S. supervision.[36] Past experience showed reporting of local election totals through these channels offered the incumbent government a tremendous advantage in the vote tabulation process. General McCoy had effectively removed this threat four years earlier. Woodward, on the other hand, seemed too engrossed in the activities going on in the Liberal party to be concerned with the complaints from Conservatives regarding general election procedures. He was more anxious to limit Moncada's influence in his party than listen to the demands of the out party. In fact, his feelings on this matter were brought out clearly when he referred to the Conservative party request by saying, "This document was calculated to embarrass the electoral mission by burdening it with the task of securing concessions and favorable action on these points from President Moncada."[37]

Moncada knew that Sacasa's victory in the party meant the beginning of his decline in Liberal party politics. The president was convinced a Sacasa election in November would be more disastrous for the Gobiernistas than a Conservative victory. Consequently, he opened negotiations with Emiliano Chamorro

---

[36] Junta Directiva Partido Conservadora to Woodward, July 8, 1932, Archivos del Tribunal Electoral Supremo, Managua.

[37] Woodward, notes on the Conservative party, July 1, 1932, RG 59, DF 817.00 Woodward/231, NA.

who knew his party had no chance of defeating the popular Sacasa. Furthermore, the veteran Conservative party leader suspected, and with good reason, Sacasa was high on the United States' list of preferred candidates. Chamorro concluded that the Conservatives stood a better chance joining forces with Moncada, so he and the president held numerous conferences planning the strategy for a political union.[38]

Even though Nicaraguan politics were somewhat characterized by rigid party discipline, members of each group had been known to cross party lines occasionally for practical reasons. Moncada had done this when he became Adolfo Díaz's minister of government in 1911. Therefore, the Liberal chieftain was not unaccustomed to making political settlements with the opposition.[39] On the ticket, the president wanted either his first choice, Antonio Barbarena, as the Liberal presidential candidate, or his later selection, Leonardo Argüello, minister of education in 1925 and president, only briefly, in 1947. He thought that a Conservative should accompany one of these candidates on the ticket. Of course, in this proposed coalition, the president would have liked his choice to run for chief executive, but he was willing to accept a vice-presidential candidate of his own on a fusion ticket. In any case, a Conservative victory meant more to him than a Sacasa triumph.[40] Chamorro made no secret of the fact that his discussions with Moncada were also based on his party's failure to raise enough money to finance a campaign. If an agreement were worked out with Moncada, he thought more lucrative financial sources could be tapped for the contest.[41]

Woodward took note of the Moncada/Chamorro deliberations and paid close attention to them for obvious reasons. But he was too preoccupied to deal with the situation directly until the plebiscite was over. Woodward was thinking in terms of a Liberal/Conservative race, not a coalition ticket. He envisioned a Conservative slate consisting of Adolfo Díaz and Emiliano Chamorro, which, in his opinion would be the

---

[38] Hanna to State Department, August 12, 1932, RG 59, DF 817.00 Woodward/131, NA. Chamorro, interview with author, Managua, April 7, 1965.

[39] RG 43, Records, 1932 mission, entry 387, NA.

[40] Woodward to State Department, n.d., RG 59, DF 817.00 Woodward/231, NA.

[41] Ibid.

strongest combination the party could put together.[42] Chamorro
had a large popular following and still was considered the real
caudillo in Nicaraguan politics. The masses idolized him, yet
with all his popular appeal, the State Department still did not
trust him. Based on past experience, they considered Díaz a
more reliable, tractable person who could be expected to
cooperate with the United States in the future, should the
Conservatives miraculously be elected.

When reporting his activities to Washington during the
crucial months just before the election, Woodward unfortunately never explained in detail how this interesting Díaz/
Chamorro ticket was created. Yet, he encouraged it in some
manner, observing that it was the best solution for a party
facing Sacasa who would be hard to beat. As chances for a
Díaz/Chamorro slate grew, money poured into the party
treasury, prompting Chamorro to end talks with Moncada. He
knew an enriched war chest greatly enhanced prospects for
victory. As a result, he devoted full time bolstering the party's
rank and file for a November contest.[43]

The Conservatives held their convention in August and,
as planned, Díaz was nominated for president with Chamorro
as his running mate. Clearly, a unique Conservative party ticket
had been created, one which Woodward and the legation were
happy to see emerge. Díaz was not present to accept his
nomination. He had left for the United States in June to raise
money for the party. In fact, the former president, like members
of the Liberal party, was to spend a great deal of time in New
York soliciting funds for his race.[44]

The U.S. Government Deals with Sandino: Reconciliation through Juan Bautista Sacasa

Sandino's military campaign had not diminished during
1932. As Woodward reported, raids had been more frequent
and effective since January of the same year than at any time
before. The United States undoubtedly wanted to end its
conflict with the rebel chief. Since President Hoover and
Stimson were determined to withdraw the marines, both
anticipated that possibly Sandino could be persuaded to

---

[42] Woodward, "Events, September to November 1932," RG 59, DF
817.00 Woodward/231, NA.

[43] Managua *El Comercio*, September 25, 1932, 1.

[44] Managua *La Noticia*, July 31, 1932.

negotiate a settlement, concluding an agreement with all Nicaraguan political parties. Unfortunately, but to no one's surprise, the rebel was determined not to conclude peace with the U.S. until the military intervention ended.

Sacasa also was anxious to terminate the Sandino war and restore the dissident Liberal's faction to the party's ranks. This would finally heal wounds dividing the party since the Tipitapa accord in 1927. Although he was confident of an electoral victory in November, Sacasa knew that he would have to deal with the rebel leader directly, without the marines' help, at some point. The Liberal standard bearer first worked to secure an agreement between the traditional parties on ways to deal with Sandino. Sacasa wanted to prevent the conclusion of any separate pacts by either Gobiernistas or Conservatives with him. If this happened, the Liberal candidate was certain it would aggravate Nicaragua's troubles by diminishing prospects for a two-party contest.[45]

In June 1932, Sacasa and Aguado drew up a proposed reconciliation plan to offer Sandino. The North American legation endorsed it but could not persuade the Triangulos to publish it. They feared if they did, it would indicate desperation on their part for votes, a sign of weakness. Hanna suggested that a third group, known as *El Grupo Patriótico* (Patriotic Group), with no political affiliation but highly respected, initiate the project. Sofonías Salvatierra, a long-time opponent of U.S. intervention, and Horacio Portocarrero, a Liberal whose lengthy exile gave him credibility among feuding local groups, headed *El Grupo Patriótico*. This body was composed of Liberals and Conservatives who had categorically opposed U.S. intervention and its war on Sandino. Consequently, Hanna thought this would be the best element to negotiate directly with the rebel in the Segovia mountains.[46] Later, Salvatierra headed a delegation to negotiate a peace settlement with Sandino. He did so and then became minister of agriculture and labor in the Sacasa government (1933-1936).

At the time Sacasa was working on an agreement with the Conservatives, a most encouraging letter, allegedly from Sandino, appeared in one of Managua's leading papers. The note was

---

[45] Hanna to State Department, Conversation with Sacasa, October 14, 1932, RG 59, DF 817.00/7582, NA.

[46] Ibid., October 14, 1932, RG 59, DF 817.00/7852, NA. On January 2, 1933, the day following Sacasa's inauguration, the last 910 marines were withdrawn from the country.

addressed to Sacasa and said in part: "I should be glad to cooperate with you in favor of national harmony and the restoration of public peace by a dignified and patriotic agreement. Speak, and perhaps we can reach an understanding."[47] U.S. government officials were encouraged by this overture as they believed Sandino was now prepared to open negotiations, albeit just with Sacasa. The Liberal candidate's victory was therefore doubly important to the North American government as it would allow the United States to make a safe, diplomatic retreat from an unpleasant, unsuccessful military intervention project.[48]

Sacasa worked to arrange for some overall agreement with the Conservatives to establish a permanent peace in the republic. First and foremost, he wanted a solution to the age-old antagonism between the parties in the country's "winner-take-all" tradition. He was certain if both Liberals and Conservatives reached a settlement in this regard, Sandino might end his rebellion and negotiate a peace. Juan Bautista Sacasa acted very much like a successful presidential candidate. Of course, he was aware that the U.S. legation welcomed his reconciliation efforts with the Conservatives and Sandino. Moreover, his victory later on and the proposed peace settlement with Sandino coincided with U.S. plans for marine withdrawal by the end of 1932. North American legation reports to the State Department clearly reflected this objective as the presidential campaign progressed.[49]

The United States wanted the 1932 elections to be supervised under an executive decree only because the Moncadistas might prevent a regulation from passing in Congress. Essentially, the proposed 1932 law was similar to the McCoy provisions in 1928 whereby North Americans would head the 13 departments and have veto power over Liberal and Conservative members on local boards. The national election board would reserve the right to canvass votes and preside over hearings dealing with disputed ballots. This was usually under the Supreme Court's jurisdiction, but the impartiality of the nation's highest tribunal had already been questioned by the United States. In any case, they asked Moncada to issue the

---

[47] Managua *El Comercio*, October 21, 1932, 1.

[48] Hanna to State Department, October 28, 1932, RG 59, DF 817.00/7698, NA.

[49] Ibid., October 14, 1932, RG 59, DF 817.00/7582, NA.

electoral decree in July. The Nicaraguan minister to the United States, Luis Manuel Debayle, reported to the State Department that President Moncada had decided to present the law to Congress anyway.

Stimson was incensed at this disregard for what he considered the implementation of an orderly election procedure and told Debayle that from this point on, "I would look to Moncada to see that the amendments were put through."[50] Obviously, the Nicaraguan minister reported the secretary's displeasure; by the end of July, Moncada issued the decree and did not wait for Congress to act. The chief executive was having enough troubles in his party and did not wish to antagonize the United States any further.[51]

Even though the United States concluded that it had only enough military personnel to supervise 182 out of 429 voting stations, numerous devices were used to assure the people that Washington intended to observe the transfer of executive power closely. As a precautionary measure, Woodward asked that the destroyer USS *Overton* be sent to Puerto Cabézas on Nicaragua's east coast. He thought this show of force would make the electorate in Bluefields, remote from the seat of the national election board in Managua, more secure in their exercise of the franchise. Moreover, the admiral also let it be known he was ready to provide "assistance" to people in Bluefields in the event Sandino decided to begin his raids there again. Preparations for using more troops from ships were made evident in a letter Woodward wrote to the commander of the Special Service Squadron: "I have...assumed that during the electoral period the employment in Nicaraguan territory of naval personnel of your command...does not differ in principle from the employment of personnel of the Second Marine Brigade of the marines....Such action is not a violation of the sovereignty of the republic of Nicaragua."[52]

Woodward realized he could not maintain control over all electoral precincts in the country. In September and early October, some one hundred fifty-four thousand people had

---

[50] Memo of conversation, Stimson and Luis Debayle, July 6, 1932, RG 59, DF 817.00/122, NA.

[51] *Decreto Ejecutivo de 1932*, n.d., Archivos del Tribunal Electoral Supremo, Managua.

[52] Woodward to Commander, Special Service Squadron, September 13, 1932, RG 43, Records, 1932 mission, entry 384, NA.

registered. On election day, November 6, the Liberals obtained a 23,000 majority vote for their candidate. Approximately eighty-four percent of those registered cast ballots electing Juan Bautista Sacasa and Rodolfo Espinosa. The election also secured Liberal party control in the national legislature. The election victory was clearly a final vindication for the new president. His unsuccessful effort as vice-president to succeed to the presidency when President Carlos Solórzano fled the country after Chamorro's coup in 1926 was finally confirmed in his victory over Díaz and Chamorro in 1932. Paradoxically, a U.S.-supervised election made this quest for political leadership a reality in 1932, four years after it negotiated a political settlement excluding Sacasa in 1928.

Once again the Conservatives put on a pitifully poor campaign. Former President Adolfo Díaz did not even appear until the day before ballots were cast.[53] The former president spent the entire summer and fall in New York seeking U.S. financial support and political endorsement. His mission failed in both respects; he was hurt that Washington did not support him in 1932 in return for his cooperation over the years and especially in 1928.[54]

Woodward was determined to have his mission succeed and have Sacasa installed as the republic's chief executive without disruption. He was not at all sure Moncada would relinquish his office. Likewise, Sandino maintained an independent military force, and the incumbent president began to fill positions in the National Guard with his party followers. A potential confrontation between these two forces was possible. Woodward viewed these developments with concern and asked permission to remain in the country indefinitely.[55] Though this plan was unwise, the U.S. withheld announcing when the marines would leave.

Admiral Woodward later offered two observations on future U.S.-run elections in a foreign territory. The first was that the U.S. government should try in every way possible to avoid commitment like the three election supervision projects in Nicaragua. Second, if it proved, in his words, "desirable or expedient for the U.S. government to again assume such a

---

[53] Managua *La Prensa*, November 3, 1932, 2.

[54] *La Noticia*, November 8, 1932, 1.

[55] Woodward to State Department, December 1, 1932, RG 43, Records, 1932 mission, entry 384, NA.

responsibility," the most absolute powers for its "electoral mission" should be ensured from the start.[56]

Shortly before the United States completed supervising the 1932 election and made plans to end the military occupation, attention turned to the selection of a National Guard commander. The United States suggested that both the Conservative and Liberal parties draw up a list for the guard's top posts. President Moncada would then appoint nominees to the positions as the victorious party proposed. In effect, this strategy ended a plan to create a nonpartisan army. President Moncada, now a bitter Sacasa foe, had successfully thwarted the latter's choice for guard commander and instead named his long-time political protegé, Anastasio Somoza Garcia, who was married to Sacasa's niece. Somoza had served as *jefe político* of León and, on different occasions, as Moncada's minister of war and deputy minister of foreign affairs. Moreover, the new guard chief, who was to take his post in January 1933, was fluent in English and had served U.S. forces well as an interpreter and in liaison tasks with the Moncada government. The departing North American military personnel and diplomatic representatives supported the appointment enthusiastically. However, Somoza's selection left incoming President Sacasa helpless in securing a cooperative, nonpartisan guard.[57]

When Sacasa was inaugurated president on New Year's Day 1933, General Calvin Matthews, head of the guard, turned over his command to the Nicaraguans. The new chief executive then proceeded with his plans to conclude a peace with Sandino who remained a significant threat to the government.[58]

On February 2, 1933, a treaty was signed that ended the rebel's military campaign. True to his word, Augusto César Sandino agreed to negotiate a peace agreement only when the last marine contingent left the country. Its main provisions were that, in return for ending his operations, the government would grant amnesty to him and his followers, provide them land, and permit them to maintain an armed force in some northern departments, particularly in the northeast Coco Valley

---

[56] *Foreign Relations* 5 (1932): 832. See also Kamman, *Search for Stability*, 216.

[57] Richard Millet, "Anastasio Somoza Garcia: A Brief History of Nicaragua's 'Enduring' Dictator." *Revista Review Interamericana* 2:3 (Autumn 1977): 489-490. See also Hanna to Secretary of State Cordell Hull, March 8, 1933, RG 59, DF 817.00/7782, NA.

[58] Ibid., 490.

and the Caribbean coast, regions where Sandinistas were given property and allowed to settle.

Significantly though, the pact did not resolve basic differences between the guard and the rebel leader's military force. Though Sandino and Somoza mutually were suspicious of each other's intentions, Sacasa vainly tried to resolve the antagonisms. Somoza insisted Sandino's forces entirely disarm one year after the agreement. This left the rebel chief determined to reduce the guard's independence.

Sandino/guard differences heightened in early 1934 when President Sacasa agreed to name a Sandinista as guard commander in the rebel-held territory. When Sandino met with President Sacasa in mid-February of the same year to resolve some basic issues in the peace agreement, the rebel leader was shot by National Guard officers with General Somoza's alleged approval.

Sandino's death clearly enhanced the power of the National Guard and its commander. Two years later, "Tacho" Somoza staged a coup d'état ousting President Sacasa. He supervised his own election, taking office in January 1937. The Somoza dynasty began its rule after the general's assassination in 1956. His sons, Luis (who died in 1967) and "Tachito" continued the reign until the family's dominance ended with a Sandinista military victory in the summer of 1979.

IX

The Legacy of Managing Democracy: 1928-1933

BY 1924, THE REPUBLIC of Nicaragua had gained control of its Pacific Railroad and National Bank from U.S. financiers who some time before had taken them over as collateral in return for loans to the country. However, North Americans held a majority on the governing boards of each enterprise until 1929. In many respects, the expansion of North American influence over the country's chief financial institutions had resulted largely from the cooperation of the nation's presidents. More often than not, in return for providing the United States with a decisive voice in the republic's fiscal management, the United States gave incumbent chief executives political support through a recognition policy and guaranteed military backing.

Domestic political conflicts in Nicaragua, specifically a civil war, were potentially dangerous in 1926 and 1927 with respect to a possible challenge to U.S. security interests in Central America. President Adolfo Díaz, for example, rightfully emphasized Mexico's support of Liberal Sacasa, raising the prospect that a Bolshevik conspiracy was, as some proclaimed, taking shape in Nicaragua. Internal strife between Conservatives and Liberals posed serious problems for the United States again, as it had over the long history of its relations with Nicaragua.

In light of Mexico's interest in Central American affairs, and as prospects emerged again in the U.S. Congress for the construction of a canal across Nicaragua, the U.S. government scrutinized that country's internal affairs closely. The age-old problem of *continuismo* also became a major issue when Emiliano Chamorro ousted the coalition government of Conservative Carlos Solórzano and Liberal Juan Bautista Sacasa and had Congress name him president in January 1926. The ousted vice president claimed to be the legal successor to Solórzano. But the United States rejected the Liberals' demands and backed (the more cooperative and pliable) Díaz for president. Liberal party leaders then began a military campaign under Sacasa to oust Díaz in 1926-1927.

The Liberal forces were determined to prevent Adolfo from remaining in office another term. Their objective was to reinstate Sacasa as the rightful successor to Solórzano. President Coolidge decided to act and demonstrate his administration's attention and concern in the matter, preempting a congressional inquiry on his administrative actions in Nicaragua.

He called upon Henry Stimson, the former secretary of war in William Howard Taft's administration, for advice as congressional opposition to the administration's Nicaraguan military intervention policy grew. At the outset, Stimson felt the U.S. should not interfere militarily in Nicaragua's political embroilments through a show of alone.

He was convinced that the country needed basic reform in its electoral process to enhance prospects for internal political peace ending civil wars. Specifically, he envisioned Nicaragua's future political stability as resting on the creation of a nonpartisan, national election board, initially headed by U.S. citizens with representation from both Liberal and Conservative parties. Stimson recommended that the United States restructure and temporarily administer Nicaragua's election machinery, thus leaving the government intact without a direct U.S. military administration. Stimson's plan was a peaceful transition of power through the electoral process between Conservative and Liberal forces.

Basically, the 1928 presidential election would be a U.S.-supervised project, unique in that Nicaragua remained ostensibly an independent state, not experiencing outright invasion with direct administration by occupying forces of North American troops as was done before in Cuba, Haiti, and the Philippines. Stimson's proposal was linked directly to U.S. chief foreign policy objectives in 1927-1928, namely the preservation of political stability in a Central American state to safeguard its wider strategic interests in the Caribbean.

Stimson's recommendation for establishing a U.S.-run Nicaraguan election board was fully implemented to the extent that the incumbent Conservative party and its presidential candidate failed to control the electoral machinery in 1928. However, in many respects, Stimson's sympathetic attitude toward José Maria Moncada assisted the Liberals considerably.

Equally significant in the 1928 Liberal party victory, Moncada's followers actively worked for a U.S.-dominated election board and similarly cooperated in every respect with the marine campaign to defeat Sandino. Liberal party leadership viewed the rebel's campaign as a serious hindrance to the voting process.

The Liberals won the 1928 presidential election largely because of the incumbent Conservative party's flagrant misuse of power. This offended the legally minded Stimson and General Frank McCoy, who in turn drastically reduced the incumbent regime's authority. Stimson never forgot that he had cooperated with him at the 1927 Tipitapa conference and frequently praised him, saying he deserved some reward. At the very least, he felt the 1928 electoral machinery would have to be managed effectively to give the Liberal standard bearer a reasonable opportunity to be elected president.

When Moncada became Nicaragua's chief executive in 1928, an era of good feeling between the United States and Nicaragua emerged, but it was short-lived. Although Stimson had a good personal relationship with Moncada, it did not insure impartially run elections in succeeding years. Nicaragua's chief magistrate was determined to strengthen both the party's apparatus and his own personal position in the 1930 congressional elections. Even though the U.S. election supervisor condemned Moncada's interference in the off-year elections, the Nicaraguan president retained Stimson's support. Yet, by 1931, the United States secretary of state realized his 1927 proposal for creating a North American-staffed national election board was rapidly losing its power to the president. Stimson was determined to fulfill the provisions of the Tipitapa agreement, which he presumably crafted, particularly the goal for creating bipartisan representation on all electoral administrative boards. However, President Moncada later refused to accept North American supervision of the 1931 municipal election. Stimson agreed, expecting the Liberal party leadership would accept an unqualified U.S.-run 1932 presidential election.

By 1932, President Moncada had successfully undermined Conservative power and influence in Congress and removed opponents from numerous local municipal posts as well. The Liberals had achieved a dominant position in the country largely through the manipulation of electoral machinery by the astute, clever Moncada, particularly after the 1928 presidential contest.

The U.S. search for a continued efficient, honest election supervision system in 1932 was clearly in jeopardy, particularly at a time when President Herbert Hoover had committed his administration to withdraw militarily from the country. The prospect of a Liberal party-run election, without constraints, was a painful one for Secretary of State Stimson. Moncada, a signatory to the Tipitapa agreement, was thwarting the principle behind the 1927 accord. Fortunately, the State Department did not have to challenge the Nicaraguan chief executive directly. The United States adopted a more subtle, less obvious tactic in its campaign to reassert a strong supervisory role in the 1932 election without Moncada's interference. Dissatisfied members of the president's party, led by Vice-President Enoc Aguado, prevented the chief executive from using the constituent assembly idea as a vehicle to extend his term of office. Admiral Clark Howell Woodward, the 1932 national election board chairman, supported Aguado. As a result, Sacasa, Stimson's personal presidential choice, was nominated in a Liberal party plebiscite.

Juan Bautista Sacasa's election in 1932 was important to the United States primarily because a negotiated peace between Sandino and the Liberal party standard bearer seemed likely. Since the Hoover/Stimson policy for final marine evacuation was set for January 1933, a conclusion to the rebel military campaign would further enhance prospects for the United States' continued influence. Sacasa realized his successful campaign was also in Washington's best interest. Consequently, he initiated efforts to stop internal strife by first ending major differences between his party and the Conservatives by drawing up an agreement that provided minority representation in Congress and in the government's executive branches. Then Sacasa proceeded to lay plans for direct negotiations with Sandino, ultimately concluding a peace agreement with him in February 1933.

U.S. election supervisors in 1932 favored the Sacasa candidacy because his election could be interpreted as the North Americans' success at preventing two incumbent presidents, Adolfo Díaz in 1928 and José Maria Moncada in 1932, from controlling electoral machinery. Moreover, Sacasa was expected to end the Sandino campaign via negotiation rather than through the U.S. Marine military campaign which had already failed in defeating the rebel. It had cost the United

States an estimated one hundred thirty-six lives. Both Moncada and Sacasa (in 1928 and 1932) based the conduct of their campaigns on the acceptance of a U.S.-run national election board. Although the two men often made direct appeals for U.S. support, they also focused their campaigns on the need to establish bipartisan-run election procedures.

The United States paid a heavy price for its involvement in the election supervision process. The Sandino movement effectively drew worldwide attention to U.S. military intervention and came close to nullifying the 1928 contest. The State Department realized that an election supervision project meant something more than simply presiding over departmental boards. It evolved into a deep and, at times, frustrating involvement in the two parties' internal conflicts.

Washington's effort to establish a bipartisan administration of election contests through equal representation on U.S.-run election boards reflected a new and unique aspect in a policy to maintain stability in Central America. Financial reform efforts and sole military intervention were eclipsed in the 1927-1933 period by attempts to recast presidential and congressional contests under the aegis of bipartisan and equally representative electoral bodies. In this period, the United States focused more attention on cutting the cost of a military campaign by promoting the free expression of the popular will.

Contrary to general belief, Liberals, with the significant exception of Augusto César Sandino, welcomed the 1928 supervision project, albeit skeptically at first. They interpreted unqualified compliance and cooperation with the national election board directives as the only chance for ousting the Conservatives in 1928. Had General McCoy not restricted Díaz' vast executive powers, the Moncada candidacy would certainly have been defeated. The Nicaraguan project was also unique in that it was not a takeover of a nation administered by United States Marines or even governing through a client state. This intervention was in many ways a new intrusion strategy. Nicaraguans would be allowed to continue ruling, but the United States would write election laws, supervise elections, and develop a nonpartisan military.

The supervised elections from 1928 to 1932 also represented a fundamental shift in the United States' attitude toward Nicaraguan political parties, particularly the Liberals. Washington was determined to see that Moncada had an opportunity to campaign unencumbered by harassments from the Conservative regime in 1928. Unofficially, the North American supervisors hoped for a Liberal party victory. On earlier occasions, the United States had supported incumbent Nicaraguan chief executives without qualification. After the first supervised election took place, the Department of State prohibited revolts by the ousted Conservatives, and this policy was particularly evident in the 1930 municipal elections.

Stimson's project for strengthening the election boards' role in political contests temporarily introduced a genuine bipartisan representation in administering election procedures. However, this was accomplished largely through U.S. personnel who exercised increasingly vast powers during the supervised elections, not from any long-range planning by President Coolidge. It was simply a different tactic, limited in scope, designed to secure United States' influence in the Caribbean, especially in light of Mexican support for Sacasa in 1927-1928 and the ensuing outbreak of a civil war.

Henry Stimson was the chief architect of the election supervision idea. He sincerely believed if bipartisan representation at all levels of election administration could be established, then dictatorship and armed uprisings would be less likely to occur. He felt that if the United States supervised a series of elections, then traditional foes, Liberals and Conservatives, would adopt the fixed guidelines for electing their national figures and end armed conflicts as a method for resolving political disputes in the process. Yet, Latin American states condemned the election supervision projects and the military intervention. Moreover, Nicaraguans resented deeply the United States meddling in their internal affairs. Sandino's assassination in 1934 eventually became a symbol of resurgent nationalism when the Sandinista Liberation Front was founded in 1962, culminating in its victory 17 years later. On the whole, most Nicaraguans directly involved in the elections accepted marine presence and election supervision. However, powerful elements, such as Sandino's armed military resistance and Emiliano Chamorro's congressional leverage, condemned the role the United States played from 1928 to 1932.

The main thrust of the United States' Nicaraguan interests clearly shifted from a single policy of direct armed intervention. Realistically, the marines were pursuing an impossible task, fighting an insurgency with no political solution. Fortunately, military intervention and election supervision from 1928 to 1933 provided the means to withdraw gracefully, recognizing

Sandino's indomitable will as a political leader and his innovative guerrilla tactics. As a result, U.S. interests in Nicaragua changed to a policy resolving domestic conflicts through election supervision, potentially ending the need for future military action. Surely, U.S. influence in the nation was not to abate. The presence of U.S. armed forces as an instrument of foreign policy was to end, being replaced by the more subtle, but significant support of the National Guard, led by Anastasio Somoza Garcia.

The United States continued to face a persistent dilemma not resolved in 1932 nor thereafter in Central America: How may Washington combine a commitment to democracy and the rule of law with respect to the sovereignty of a state and, at the same time, preserve its security interests? The long Somoza era that followed this intervention, however innovative in approach, attests to the preeminence of the latter goal.

Historically, Nicaragua has perhaps been the most overt of the Central American countries in demonstrating its nationalist feelings — mostly because its narrow strip of land, lanes connecting the Atlantic and Pacific, make it of prime importance.

Repeated interventions throughout its history have created a pantheon of heroes. The United States created one in the 1927 intervention, and his legacy provided the basis for a Sandinista revolution in 1979.

Bibliographical Essay

In preparing this work, the author examined several major sources both in Nicaragua and the United States. The Records of the Supreme Electoral Tribunal and its sessions, 1927-1932, in Managua's National Archives and documents in the Ministerio de Gobernacíon provided excellent and detailed accounts of the Liberal and Conservative party deliberations on election administration. Unfortunately, most of these materials were destroyed in the Managua earthquake in 1972. This source offered insights on factional disputes within the major political parties as well. These internal feuds allowed U.S. election supervisors the opportunity to mediate disputes — sometimes by casting votes on procedural matters, wielding great power on the selection of party candidates at the national and local levels. In Washington, the entire records of the United States Electoral Missions from 1928 to 1932 are in the National Archives. This substantial collection contains documents on election supervision not only for Nicaragua's presidential contests in 1928 and 1932 but also congressional and municipal elections in 1930 and 1931.

The private papers of U.S. Election Board Chairman Frank Ross McCoy, housed in the Manuscript Division of the Library of Congress, provided considerable personal insights on the administration of the 1928 election — especially correspondence outside official channels to Stimson and candid appraisals of events to close friends and family members. They shed light, too, on the intra-service rivalry of North American marine, army, and navy forces on Nicaraguan political matters and the training of the National Guard. Diplomatic and consular dispatches in the Washington National Archives offered insightful political reports from many small towns and regions in Nicaragua to the United States legation on election matters. These documents, known as post dispatches, were in turn incorporated in diplomatic reports from United States ministers to the Department of State. Copies and some original marine corps records dealing with the Sandino movement and its impact are also in the National Election Board Records. Although the marine corps documents are not central to this work covering one aspect of the United States intervention, they provided excellent insight on local, municipal, and political issues during the election supervision proceedings. The Henry L. Stimson Diary and Papers in the Yale Library rendered significant perspectives on the foundation and stated objectives of a U.S. ruling from 1928-1932 which created the framework for election supervision and the establishment of a non-political military force. Stimson's diary and papers also offered an excellent glimpse — a panorama of personal, family, and political rivalries — into Nicaragua's political culture during the civil war in 1927.

The author also interviewed many old Sandino followers in northern Nicaragua, where the major part of the rebel campaign was conducted. However, the most insightful of these personal accounts were the numerous conversations with the late President Emiliano Chamorro. His views and thoughts on Nicaraguan political issues and personalities, as well as his long and contentious relations with the United States, were elicited in several discussions. While Sandino led the rebel military campaign against the United States, Chamorro worked prodigiously and effectively, using legal strategies to end U.S. intervention. As president on several occasions and as a member of Congress, he was a dominant force in the Conservative party. He successfully raised constitutional issues to show the contradiction in the use of arbitrary, capricious measures under the guise of the law to promote democracy in his country through election supervision.

Several first-hand accounts of the election project were published by Nicaraguans during and after the intervention (1928-1933). Among them was President Moncada. Some of his notes and papers were published in 1930. Yet members of Moncada's family, especially his son, provided additional unpublished material to the author dealing with many political matters during the civil war in 1927 and later in his father's term as chief executive (1928-1932).

Many leading political figures such as Adolfo Díaz, Emiliano Chamorro, and Carlos Cuadra Pasos published their autobiographies in article-length pieces in Managua's *Revista*

Conservadora del Pensamiento Centro Americano. This jour-
nal, renamed *Revista del Pensamiento Centro Americano*, is a
rich archive on the lives of these Nicaraguan politicians,
particularly their activities during the intervention period,
1928-1934.

Still the major and standard secondary source on the 1925-
1933 period of U.S. interests — economic, political, and
military — in Nicaragua is William Kamman's, *A Search for
Stability: United States Diplomacy Toward Nicaragua, 1925-
1933* (University of Notre Dame Press, 1968). A. J. Bacevich's
biography of General McCoy, *Diplomat in Khaki: Major
General Frank Ross McCoy and American Foreign Policy,
1898-1949* (University of Kansas Press, 1989), gives a fine
overview of General Leonard Wood's protegé in many assignments abroad, including Nicaragua in 1928. Neill Macaulay's
The Sandino Affair provides the best account of Sandino's life
and military campaign against the United States, from 1927 to
1933. For a more detailed listing of these sources and others,
especially the political aspects of U.S. intervention through
supervised presidential elections in 1928 and 1932, see the
author's *United States in Nicaraguan Politics, 1927-1933* (Ph.D.
diss., George Washington University, 1966).

About the Author

Thomas J. Dodd is on the faculty of the Edmund A. Walsh School of Foreign Service, Georgetown University, and teaches Latin American history and diplomacy. He also has chaired the advanced seminar, Central America and the Spanish Caribbean, Foreign Service Institute, U.S. Department of State. His books include *The Letters of Tomas Herrán: Colombian Diplomat*, *The Panama Crisis 1900-1903*, and (co-authored) *Latin American Foreign Policies.*